Letters to J. D. Salinger

Letters to
J. D. Salinger

EDITED BY
CHRIS KUBICA AND WILL HOCHMAN

THE UNIVERSITY OF WISCONSIN PRESS

The University of Wisconsin Press
1930 Monroe Street
Madison, Wisconsin 53711

www.wisc.edu/wisconsinpress/

3 Henrietta Street
London WC2E 8LU, England

5   4   3   2   1

Printed in the United States of America

Library of Congress Cataloging-in-Publication Data
Letters to J.D. Salinger / edited by Chris Kubica and Will Hochman.
   pp.   cm.
   ISBN 0-299-17800-5 (cloth: alk. paper)
   1. Salinger, J. D. (Jerome David), 1919– Correspondence.
2. Authors and readers—United States. 3. Authorship.
I. Kubica, Chris. II. Hochman, Will.
PS3537.A426 Z48   2002
813'.54—dc21   2001006770

Contents

PART TWO   Students & Teachers

PART THREE   From the Web

Acknowledgments

Chris Kubica wishes to offer many thanks and all his love to Wendy (a.k.a. Sparkler), his wonderful, one-of-a-kind wife. Without her love, good humor, and understanding, this book would not have been possible. He'd also like to thank Mr. Horan, *genius domus* of Huntley Elementary School, who introduced him to the value and amusement of keeping one's nose in books.

Introduction

Dear Reader,

My love affair with the U.S. mail began in fourth grade shortly after I read my first comic book during recess. It wasn't a very exciting story. Completely forgettable, actually, but on the comic's inside back cover was a colorful series of advertisements through which a grade school lad with a few bucks could buy many wondrous, valuable, and sparkly things: pills that could make you strong-man-muscular in under three weeks, a space-age coin-counting device, an ant farm made out of a mysterious high-impact polymer, and rare, uncanceled stamps from Africa and the Middle East. I began sending away for anything and everything, using up a fair amount of my spare time. I decided at age eleven (because of the large volume of mail I was now generating) that I needed my own return address labels, which I ordered from an ad found in the coupon section of the Sunday *Post-Crescent*, Appleton, Wisconsin's local newspaper. I also bought a box of glue sticks to expedite the sealing of envelopes.

Rarely did the items I ordered ever turn out to be just what I'd *hoped* they'd be. The coin-counting device, for example, was nothing more than a flat, black plastic tray with half-circle grooves molded into it, each groove with tiny, barely visible raised numbers running along its sides. And those X-ray glasses only allowed me a brief glimpse behind the many silly ads I'd been answering. But the thrill of creatively and rapidly composing correspondence ("Why yes, thanks for asking, I'd love to be one of the first to try a pack of your riotous, red pepper gum!"), waiting six to eight weeks and then, at last, opening the mailbox to find small, liberally taped packages from far-off places like Ohio was always worth it. Some days, and with increasing regularity, I'd get more mail than my mother. And on those dismal days when we got *no* mail at all, I'd plead with Mom to drive me down to the Post Office to see if there'd been some mistake, to see if there was some little lawn care equipment magazine or homeowner's insurance flier waiting for me.

In a junior high English class, I was taught how to write proper letters of praise and complaint. I used this skill to send away for free — but this time more useful — stuff. It seemed that whether I complained about a product or congratulated the hell out of it, companies, at least at that time, had more coupons than they knew what to do with lying around the office and were more than willing to send them to anyone who had a stamp and *anything* at all to say about their stuff. I got three free cases of Pepsi this way — three months in a row — not to mention a bunch of free BASF-brand cassette tapes and enough mini-toothpastes to fill an entire bathroom drawer.

As I began to grow weary of the limited number of pencils and paper stocks available at the one small drug store that was a bike ride from my house, I tried to come up with ways to make enough money to buy a ticket to somewhere — anywhere — that offered a bigger selection. During a visit to my great-grandmother, Chicago became a contender when I checked out the "Stationers" heading in her Yellow Pages. Truthfully, though, any city large enough to be printed on my old globe would have suited me just fine. I thought maybe I could *invent* something to make some quick traveling cash; one idea I dreamed up was for a new kind of cigarette lighter made of glue, a spring, a tongue depressor, and a box of matches. I also drew up plans for a new board game tentatively called "The Dark Ages" which was kind of like chess but with a ten by ten board and two extra pieces called the Wizards who could move in all the same directions as the Queen but only three squares at a time. I tried to sell these ideas to a company I think was called Inventors International, Inc., another back-of-the-comic book ad-placer. For $1,200 a pop they would have helped me come up with winning marketing plans and I would have made more than enough dough to finally get out of town, but my weekly allowance at the time was only $2.00.

When high school began, after it sunk in that a fancy pen and paper quest in the big city wasn't going to be a financial reality for me, I tried to get to know some of the people I sat next to every day in my acting and drawing classes. I struck up a correspondence with one classmate from art class who was an excellent cartoonist. Between classes we'd exchange hastily scribbled notes and drawings with each other by folding then jamming them through the narrow vent-slats of our locker doors. Bryan, another friend who was on an exchange program to Costa Rica for the year, sent to me and received from me at *least* one letter a day, sometimes more than one. I can't remember how much money I spent on stamps but I think perhaps too much. Every day I'd come home from school and take that day's "Bryan letter" — filled with details of Bryan's latest adventures, like almost falling over the rim into an active volcano or haggling angrily over the price of a cheap necklace in downtown San José — out of the mailbox and put it in my backpack to read in my less-than-exciting Environmental Science class. Around late junior year, I started to get letters from universities I had applied to. I even corresponded briefly with the Navy ROTC program but was not successful in my attempts to convince them that they would benefit from my interest in creative writing.

Early in my senior year I first read *The Catcher in the Rye* and started saying "if you want to know the truth" at the end of my sentences. During second semester I read the rest of Salinger's books and some of his uncollected stories at the local public library and realized that Salinger's characters were also quite fond of sending and receiving mail.

During college at the University of Minnesota I wrote mostly long, gloomy letters to myself and killed time by building makeshift furniture out of my *New Yorker* subscription in my dorm room. I corresponded briefly with a girl I liked in high school but never talked to because I thought I was too inexperienced. In one letter she wrote that she'd had a serious crush on me for a long time and wondered, "Why didn't you ever ask me out on a date?"

After college, I relocated to Madison, Wisconsin, became an office temp and typed someone *else's* letters all day while at night, in the apartment I shared with two old friends, I wrote letters to famous people who, for some reason, I found it very easy to connect with. But I didn't write fan letters.

Famous people don't really respond to fan letters, at least not in my experience. No, there was a better way to inspire a response than by trying to get
through the usual front door. I decided that I'd simply send a brief letter of
introduction, followed by three poems that I'd recently written. "No reply
necessary. Just wrote to say 'Hello!' and to share some of my writing with
you." I did my first manually-assembled mass mailing, sending hundreds
and hundreds of these letters all over the world to, among others, United
States governors, the president of the United States and leaders of approximately one hundred other foreign countries, and the CEOs from
most but not all of the *Fortune* 500 companies. Before long, and much
to my amazement, responses came pouring in. The prime minister of
Jamaica wrote to me that my letter and poems were "a welcome break in
an otherwise very busy day." The CEO of Merrill Lynch and the governor
of Oregon liked the poems I sent about drinking hot chocolate and about
fishing, respectively, and I began to feel strangely invigorated by all these
letters from important people regarding such relatively unimportant
matters.

In 1995 I attended Columbia College's fiction writing program in Chicago
where I was finally able to pay my respects to a good number of those pen
and paper stores I'd always wanted to visit. I also started to become more
than just casually interested with all things Salinger. Like so many of this
book's contributors, I sought out and read every last word written by and
about Salinger. I also resolved to pick up a local copy of *The Catcher in
the Rye* from a bookshop in every country I visited in my life. (*Il Giovane
Holden* just came home with me from a trip to Italy.) At one point, I even
planned a pilgrimage to Salinger's house, though thankfully I never made
the drive. Instead I started composing a letter to the most famous literary
recluse which I planned and outlined, then wrote and rewrote. But I never
really knew what to say. I'd read many articles about people writing to
Salinger or trying to see and talk to him in person and how he got upset
and sometimes semiviolent toward them. Salinger didn't always seem like
a very pleasant person, and I didn't want to get snubbed or be bothersome.
But what, I wondered while literally thumbing my chin, was Salinger's

back door? In what way might he actually appreciate being contacted? I thought about it for weeks, but drew a blank.

The pivotal event of this period, at least as it relates to *Letters to J. D. Salinger*, was in early 1995 when I read W. P. Kinsella's *Shoeless Joe*. In the book, the main character, Ray Kinsella, kidnaps J. D. Salinger and takes him to a baseball game, among other places. "Hey," I thought, "This Kinsella is my kind of writer." Not at *all* because I'd thought of or would approve of anyone doing such a terrible thing to dear old Mr. Salinger, but because it was clear that Kinsella was moved by and greatly admired Salinger's work and at least in some small way was attempting to connect with the man through a fictional "back door." I bought several of Kinsella's other books and read them one after the other. One of them is called *The Alligator Report* and in its introduction Kinsella tells us that the book is dedicated to and written in the style of Richard Brautigan, a deceased poet and another one of *my* favorite writers (as well as Kinsella's biggest influence). Kinsella goes on to tell us how, like Holden Caulfield, he always wanted to shake his favorite author's hand and how he even tried to call Brautigan up on the phone once to tell him how much he enjoyed his work. Then Kinsella does something that I still think is brilliant — and important, with respect to *this* book — he reprints a letter that he wrote to Brautigan several years earlier, in 1980, preceded by the following passage: "Though he must have received thousands like it, I'm glad I wrote, I'm glad I let him know how he touched my life. I'm only sorry that it wasn't enough, that I couldn't have done more." It was at this moment that I thought about how many other people — famous writers or otherwise — had a letter to Brautigan in them or had already written to Brautigan, and what did those letters say? I also wondered how many people — famous writers or otherwise — had written or wanted to write a letter to *other* authors that I had read and admired over the years, like for instance J. D. Salinger.

In late 1995 I started to do some research on the Internet and found out that there were many — from the United States to Iran to India to Korea and back again — who seemed interested in not only reaching out to Salinger but in exchanging ideas with other readers about Salinger's works and literary craft. ("Let's talk about the symbolism of the gloves in CITR. SOMEONE PLEASE REPLY!!!!!!" is one of many Web bulletin board posts I'd seen.) I also discovered that there are quite a few very well known writers, scholars, entertainers, and others who publicly consider Salinger to be one of their favorite writers or a significant inspiration (Matt Groening, Ethan Hawke, Winona Ryder, and Bill Gates, to name a few). Some had even sent Salinger a letter, though most, to my knowledge, got no reply.

In 1997, in my spare time, I ran a small literary magazine called *spelunker flophouse* with my then girlfriend (now wife) Wendy, a former pen pal to whom I had sent love letters for over a year. As poetry editor and assistant short fiction editor, I compiled a database of the addresses of the writers I most admired and wrote flattering letters to them soliciting fiction or poetry for the magazine. I also wrote these same writers asking them if they had ever thought about writing a letter to Salinger. I asked, How has Salinger's work influenced you or your writing? Did you ever wonder about some of the choices Salinger made in terms of character, dialogue, or plot? What did you wonder? Would you consider publishing a letter to Salinger in a collection of such letters for all of us to read and to save it, in effect, from Salinger's nearest landfill? As word spread on the Internet and as I sent out more and more letters to potential contributors over the course of the next five years, I gathered these letters to Salinger together into a manuscript and it became the book that you now hold. It's been a long road from my first comic book letters, but worth every paper cut, every trip to the Post Office, every stamp.

Letters to J. D. Salinger is divided into three sections. In the Writers & Readers letters you'll find, among many other things, pure creative exercises, humorous ponderings, letters containing comments and questions on Salinger's craft, and letters that wonder aloud about how Salinger's personae and publications have shaped creative writers and creative writing over the course of the last fifty-or-so years. The letters in Students & Teachers are of a generally more academic nature and most, but not all, are written by folks actively studying American literature, though many of these letters also reveal how Salinger's works have deeply and irreversibly affected people's lives from both the master- and apprentice-of-literature point of view. Yes, there are letters (and contributors) in this book that defy classification in either of these first two sections (certainly a young writer like Don de Grazia must consider himself a writer, reader, student, *and* teacher) but I think you'll find that the arrangement of letters into these two cabinets is apt.

In From the Web you will find a sampling of energetic posts from my jdsalinger.com Web site. These letters run the gamut from silly, random and off-the-beaten-path to irreverent, rambling, and hopelessly devoted. Letters in this section have been left virtually unedited to give you the truest possible flavor of a typical post to a Web "guest book," bad grammar, excessive exclamation points, and emoticons (those little smiley faces you can make with colons and parentheses) included.

The book concludes with Will Hochman's Postscript, which analyzes how the Web has created a new space in the digital age for nonscholars to respond to literature. Hochman also discusses how these lay opinions are just as important but significantly different from traditional printed scholarship. I think you'll see that this is just one of many good reasons for setting letters to Salinger from Internet users apart from the rest of the letters in the book. (Another is that it can help English teachers who are interested in using this book in a classroom situation to zero in on letters that are most relevant for students in particular literature courses.)

A note on the letter gathering and selection processes: In addition to the solicitation that I sent out to several hundred noted authors which I mentioned earlier, I mass e-mailed an open call for letters to be printed out and posted on university English department bulletin boards. I also created the jdsalinger.com Web site and advertised it on Internet search engines and on the Bananafish Usenet discussion group. When selecting letters, my goal was to find as many original voices and diverse perspectives as possible, with an emphasis on "original voices." Thus, you will find few letters written as if from the hand of Holden Caulfield (though every contributor seems to nod, each in his or her own way, to some favorite small piece of Salingeria). You *will* however find letters written from almost every imaginable point of view (ethnic background, socio-economic class, geographic location, age, level of education, taste in literature . . . you name it, it's here).

People sometimes ask me, what's the whole point? Why even bother with all this? If Salinger ever hears about this book he won't read it. And if someone sends him a copy he's likely to use it as kindling or drop it into his Post Office's circular file on the way out the door. My answer is simple: This book isn't for Salinger. It's for me. And for you. And for anyone who has read and been touched by Salinger's words and wants to find out what everyone *else* thinks about them. Since about 1965, Salinger has "checked out" from public life, leaving our many questions about his life and his works unanswered. This book provides a forum for these questions, thoughts, and creative ponderings. Before you ask, no I don't expect Salinger to respond to any of these letters. The letters contained herein are for the *rest* of us to read, digest, and respond to. Salinger has already written many fine letters to us in the form of short stories and a novel about a kid from New York City who misses everybody. *Letters to J. D. Salinger* is really our collective response to *his letters*.

I imagine this book as a sort of shadow (or readers') biography of Salinger. Stand all the letters in this book edge-up in a circle. Project from behind the letters a white light and observe where the words and ideas from each letter intersect (or diverge for that matter) within the circle. Warren French once lived down the street from Salinger but ended up feeling rather distant from him, while Sid Salinger lived on the other side of the country yet felt a close, familial connection. In semirural southern California in the 1970s, *The Catcher in the Rye* passed Cris Mazza's "relevant" test, while in a small Paris hotel room in 2001, Barry Silesky's fourteen-year-old son thought the same book was simply "great." If you stare into this reading and writing tableau long enough, you'll begin to make out an image — one that coalesces and rises up from these pages like the illusion in a random-dot stereogram — of Jerry Salinger the boy becoming the man, Private Salinger the war veteran, and J. D. Salinger the legendary but reclusive American author. You'll also see the silhouette of the many writers, readers, students, and teachers who were gracious enough to express these personal thoughts.

Happily, I've discovered that many of the writers in this book have the same nostalgic passion for mailed correspondence that I had as a kid and that most succeed, with greater ease than me, in preserving their old, time-consuming ways of writing letters to people. John McFarland, for example, sends artful, humorous postcards. His printing is much more orderly-looking than mine. Warren French once proudly typed "No fax. No E-mail." at the end of a letter sent to me composed on what appears to be a very difficult to operate typewriter. (He's also not shy with the Liquid Paper.) The original of Molly Peacock's letter to Salinger, and all of her letters to me, are handwritten in the light brown ink of what I hope is an antique fountain pen.

As for me, the only handwriting I do anymore is on birthday cards and forms — like the medical history forms at my doctor's office and the "creative visualization" forms in my *The Relaxation & Stress Reduction Workbook*. The only letters I type, print, and stick stamps on now are of an official nature — letters to my publisher, letters to clients at work, letters to the local newspaper regarding an ad for an old computer I'm trying to sell. And when I open the mailbox in front of my house I'm usually greeted by spiders, bills, and credit card offers. But every once in a while I'll still get a piece of junk mail from a novelty company that has kept up with all of my address changes over the years. Every once in a while I'll order something.

I've become consumed with this semi-new form of correspondence called e-mail, sending sometimes more than fifty a day. I love swapping short stories with my friend who's in rabbinical school in Israel while discussing the odds of winning the lottery with my old friend Bryan in Minnesota while receiving digital pictures of my niece and nephew from my mother in Wisconsin — all simultaneously, all with the same electronic in- and out-boxes. I always respond immediately, typing as fast as I can, often completely disregarding proper punctuation, grammar, and paragraph breaks. At least the computer checks my spelling when I click the send button (though it always asks that I replace my last name with "cubicle"). Since my hands are never as fast as my mind would like them to be, I'm saving up to buy a new, speedy desktop computer and some speech recognition software that I hope will be able to keep up with my dictated thoughts while allowing me to stay as physically connected — but with my voice instead of with my fingers — to my letters and their recipients as I can. On this new journey, my last name will continue to bring joy — the only piece of speech recognition software I've tested thus far fared well but offered "Cub ink on" when I said "Kubica."

Please feel free to post *your* letter to Salinger at <www.jdsalinger.com>. We'll all read them.

With respect and admiration for everyone who has contributed to this collection,

> *Sincerely yours,*
> *Chris Kubica*

PART ONE

Writers & Readers

"If only you'd remember before ever you sit down to write that you've been a *reader* long before you were ever a writer. You simply fix that fact in your mind, then sit very still and ask yourself, as a reader, what piece of writing in all the world Buddy Glass would most want to read if he had his heart's choice. The next step is terrible, but so simple I can hardly believe it as I write it. You just sit down shamelessly and write the thing yourself."

—J. D. Salinger, *Seymour: An Introduction*

Dear Salinger:

All these salutes! Raise high the roof beams! Shoot the fireworks! Hardly a reader among our generation to whom Holden Caulfield didn't speak, even those of us for whom a prep school was a place we had scarcely heard of, let alone attended. And after fifty years his story still has the power to lead us along, the power of his voice. The most famous literary adolescent since Huck Finn old Holden was. Is.

And if when we first read the book we responded mainly to certain resonances, the slurs against the feeling of youth, the affronts against the world's decorum, the maddening solitude of the misunderstood soul, the horror of hypocrisy, and the putting on of airs, and now when we reread it, after decades and decades of deep reading and deep living, neither of which activities is entirely free of pain, we see the underlying patterns, the initiation tale at work, the obstacles confronting our young hero with his signature red hunting cap turned backward singling him out in the crowd, the various labors he must perform in order to achieve completion of his mission, and how vexed most of his labors become, the tortured trial of sex, the quest for whisky, carrying "Little Shirley Beans" into the dark wood of Central Park only to drop and shatter it.

A good book is one that you can read more than once and a great book may be one that you can read once in youth and once in middle age and then perhaps again in old age and find that it holds together for you. A few more decades and we may try it again, and if you're still around we'll prob-ably send the laurel wreath. But let's leave analysis to the critics. I have a few dark words.

At Rutgers, in New Brunswick, New Jersey, a few of us would-be writers once staked out the university library stacks where the *New Yorker* maga-zine was stored, waiting for your latest stories to appear. It never occurred to us to buy the magazine. And when the issue with a new story of yours would arrive, we would stealthily razor out the pages and keep them for our own. We felt such an empathy for your fiction we believed that your stories belonged to us! To think now how sweet and stupid we were, cutting out the pages and cutting your audience from you!

But decades and decades later some symmetry shows through. All these years that we've been waiting for new work from you. And what have you done but cut off your audience from new work? Taken a razor to time. Some of us are angry, maestro, and you may not care. But I'm here to vent. Talk about bad stewardships! You've cut us off from only you know how many thousands of pages of new fiction, pages which, unless you burn them yourself or mandate a bonfire at your demise, will eventually find their way into print.

You must either be the happiest writer on earth, or the craziest! And I'm voting for the former, since at least one of us should benefit from this long silence.

Alan Cheuse

🦋   Alan Cheuse is the author of a number of novels and story collections including *The Light Possessed* and *Lost and Old Rivers.* He is also a regular commentator on National Public Radio. He lives in Washington, D.C.

Dear J. D. Salinger:

First things first. How best to address you? Dear Mr. Salinger seems wrong, Dear Salinger presumptuous; I wouldn't write Dear Dostoevski or Dear Mr. Sterne. Your initials establish our distance already, your nickname or nicknames pretend to a friendship I alas can't claim. It's a little like the way that poet named himself, the one with two capitalized first letters and a trisyllabic patronymic who wrote the libretto for *Cats*. I mean young Tommy Eliot. Or should we call him Tom? At any rate and after due deliberation (of the Eliotic kind that might have occupied your Seymour until he established a way to proceed) I've settled on the way you name yourself in print: Dear J. D. it was and will be . . .

Nor do the letters *to* you cause attention lately; it's the letters *from*. What we send you doesn't matter much; what you send by way of answer fetches thousands on the auction block and occasions a ruckus to boot. So I don't expect a response. In some ways your silence determines our speech; it has come to feel more sounding, *re*-sounding that any sort of interview or any pages published could have been. What you refuse to engage in is the getting and spending that most of us live by — these very lines, for example, this simulacrum of talk.

And yet somehow that silence (though we're told you keep on writing) has preserved the work. Scarab-like and fixed in their own amber, your books defy such metaphor and have the literal last word. No need to reconsider *Franny and Zooey*, say, in the light of more recent additions; the Glass house stands intact. We have acquired no new stones to throw at it, no further instructions for that carpenter to modify the roof beam, no alterations after the fact. It stays a constant weather for bananafish, an unaltered Connecticut landscape through which Uncle Wiggily wanders, the same Central Park for Holden; it simply doesn't change. And that's why what seems dated on the page defies the calendrical pedant; you're not tarting up or lifting face or letting your characters age. A good working definition of lastingness, J. D.; the stories and the novel and novellas are what they were and will be.

Like you I'm drawn to brevity and prey to distraction, long-windedness; in your honor I'll keep these lines brief. More and more it seems that Ezra Pound was right: *What thou lovest well remains, the rest is dross.* Goodnight. And do please know how much we honor you, how much of a difference you made.

N. F. Delbanco

Nicholas Delbanco has written twenty books including novels, collections of stories, and nonfiction works. He directs the MFA program in creative writing at the University of Michigan, Ann Arbor.

J—

Speculation is all around us, so why not indulge in a little of it ourselves? If this were a large picture postcard, not a letter tucked away between the covers of this book, a photograph on the picture side could very well show this:

An earnest nineteen-year-old youth sits ramrod straight in a vinyl high-backed seat of a Greyhound bus. He is wearing a blue-and-white-striped seersucker jacket, a yellow button-down dress shirt, and tortoise-shell glasses. Behind the lenses, his eyes reveal a fellow perpetually agog at whatever strange and wonderful events confront him, a quality that makes him a good audience and an excellent listener. He has lips that beg to be kissed and maybe they will be as soon as he reaches his destination. He is an innocent, though not dumb, and, like all people his age, he is hungry for adventure. On his lap sits a paperback edition of *The Catcher in the Rye*.

And on the side of the postcard reserved for writing, the message would be:

> May 26, 1962
> Dear Mr. Salinger,
> Final exams are over and I'm headed to Chicago to see my girl-friend. No more physics labs! Not a slide rule in sight until September! For the ride from Boston, I brought along some books and I'm reading yours first. I love it, but what kind of fool wouldn't?
> A while back, I was getting the funny feeling that the elderly woman sitting next to me was reading over my shoulder. Just to make sure that she wouldn't get a load of more than she could handle, though, I tilted the book away from her and hoped that she'd respect that reading should be a private experience. But as I read on, I could still sense her eyes boring in on me.
> Finally, I spread my hands over both pages and looked up. I met her eyes. She seemed very sweet, an eager little bird. I smiled.

She smiled back. "Are you a student?" she asked.

"Yes," I replied, "I go to MIT."

"Oh," she said, "I don't know that, but then I wouldn't because, you see, I live in Buffalo."

"It's in Massachusetts," I said and smiled.

"That's nice," she said.

After that exchange I returned to Holden's adventures fulltime and my seatmate was content to look at the scenery (Ohio). She has no idea what she's missing. What would life be like if every time you found yourself faced by your own ignorance, you could excuse it away because of where you lived? I know that if I put that kind of answer down on any of my exams, I wouldn't need the return half of this bus ticket, let me tell you. By the way, I feel as if Holden is right here on the bus ride with me, a companion of the very best water. Thanks.

Your big fan,

John

Now, if I'd actually written and sent this card instead of merely relating the tale to my friend *and* if its arrival had disarmed you, you might have responded with a few words on a smaller postcard showing a mountain view. You might even have written that you, I, and others in our weaker moments may think that we'd like to hide out in a land of blissful ignorance, but, because of who we are, we have no other choice than to shoulder the burden of what we see before us. You could have gone on to say that we are compelled to learn what we do not already know and apply all that we do know because that is the honorable contract between every conscious being and the complex world in which we live. I would have treasured this card as a personal connection *and* I would have appreciated hearing so early on what took me years to learn by myself.

In the course of that 1962 bus ride, Holden Caulfield became one of my secret sharers. Over time I've discovered that I am not the only person who has adopted one of your characters as a boon nonhuman companion. One summer, while I was working for the U.S. Treasury Department in

Washington, I met a woman who regarded Franny as her best friend. Their intimacy was so intense that the woman insisted that she knew why Franny had fainted. She informed me that she had had the same experience and assured me that Franny had been overcome by a spiritual crisis. Who was I to argue with Franny's best friend, a person with no reason to make this up?

Years later in Seattle, I met a woman who was beginning to edit a book review insert for a newspaper. When Susan and I got around to discussing business, I let her know that I only had time to do brief reviews because I had to dedicate most of my writing energy to finishing up my first book.

"Who is bringing it out?" she asked.

When I said, "Little, Brown," she fell on the floor in awe. "They published my all-time favorite novel!"

"Oh," I said.

"*The Catcher in the Rye*. I read it once a year. Religiously," she said. "Good old Phoebe. It's like with my brother and me."

I had no choice but to tell her my Greyhound story.

"Every time I've been in Buffalo, I've had a curious sensation of having my brain emptied out and now I understand," she said.

Susan's ritual revisiting of *The Catcher in the Rye* spurred me on to do the same. Each time I read it, I renew my fondness for Holden, such a brave and true youth, and I feel as if a close, close friend has come for a long-overdue visit. For days after finishing the novel, I continue to feel his presence. As I go from place to place, doing battle with all the details of daily life, I find myself storing up impressions to share with Holden later when we are in private. The miracle of afterglow.

One example will give you an idea. Soon after one of my most recent readings of *The Catcher in the Rye*, I went to a screening of *Paris Is Burning*, a documentary about drag balls in Harlem, a film packed to the rafters with vamping and prancing in the most elaborate costumes and makeup. The idea behind these balls is to create an illusion and to *win*, to be judged the best at the chosen illusion. Now, keep in mind that these are grown men of limited means who dedicate enormous energy and resources to this pursuit. Granted, some of the results are visually quite breathtaking, but I ask you the simple question: Why?

A particularly thought-provoking portion of the documentary is devoted to the concept of "realness." In contrast to the main event of the drag balls where the point is to look like the most glamorous thing that ever escaped from a Vegas floor show, this section of the competition focuses on the construction of a "real life" look and the attitude adopted in carrying off that illusion. The prize goes to the man who convinces that the illusion is "real," not the contrivance it is. One after another, men troop out duded up in junior executive drag, army sergeant drag, college student drag, psychiatrist drag, computer nerd drag.

Mesmerized and unnerved by the fantastic parade on the screen, I pondered the exchange that Holden and I could have about this documentary. Although we'd have to agree that the filmmaker presented what the men were doing as harmless fun, this spectacle of men dedicating vast amounts of energy to sheer illusion was unbearably sad to me. Emotional responses aside, we'd also have to admit that what we have here is not out of step with the mainstream in a time when too many routinely claim to have degrees from schools they never even applied to and circulate résumés fraudulently claiming one outlandish achievement after another. It's enough to make you weep. It's enough to make you check into an out-of-the-way motel in Buffalo for a good, long rest.

When Little, Brown did bring out my book at long last, I could finally emerge from the sad confines of movie theaters and the stimulation of imaginary conversations to find myself at all the gigs associated with present-day book promotion. At the tail end of these events, strangers march right up and introduce themselves. "Nice to meet you," I always say. What else can you say to a stranger? That is never the end of it, as you well know.

Like clockwork, one or more of them will announce, "I'm a writer too."

The first time this happened, I was excited to meet my peers since I wanted to hear *their* war stories. "Oh, really," I replied. "What do you write?"

I was stunned when the person said, "I haven't actually written anything down yet, but I have terrific ideas."

As this scene repeated itself at every stop, I developed a way to deal with the situation. It worked so well that I use it to this very day. When a stranger approaches me with that familiar look and proudly proclaims that he or she is a writer, I simply ask, "Are you J. D. Salinger?" It stops them cold.

You'll be relieved to know that nobody yet has claimed to be you. They may be strangers and they may be presumptuous, but they all appear to be honest. I do hope for that day when I hear an affirmative response to my stock question and can then thank you in person for all the pleasure your work has brought and continues to bring to me. Until that time, this letter that stands in for the unwritten postcard of May 1962 will have to do.

With warmest regards,
John McFarland

❧   John McFarland is the author of *The Exploding Frog and Other Fables from Aesop*. His short fiction, essays, and criticism have appeared in many journals and anthologies, including *The Isherwood Century: Essays on the Life and Work of Christopher Isherwood*. He lives in Seattle, Washington.

To Whom It May Concern;

No, I won't even cause you the pain I assume I would by addressing you by name, even in a letter I doubt very much you will ever read.

Dear Sir;

What right do I have, in any case, to address you at all? And in public, no less. I apologize for the unthinking intrusion. Perhaps I should have declined Chris Kubica's request to contribute to this book. But at this point in a still-young career, I don't quite have the guts to deny myself the opportunity to publish, especially among such esteemed colleagues, even at the expense of my good sense and dignity, not to mention at the expense of yours.

Dear Occupant;

For reasons that remain obscure, I've been thinking lately about Cat Stevens, the British pop star who, after a highly successful career in the 1970s ("Moonshadow," "Peace Train," remember?), embraced a strict form of Islam that forbids its adherents to play musical instruments. Consequently, he dropped out of public life, he changed his name to Yusuf Islam and turned his back on a vulgar secular world and a music business more interested in commodity than in art.

Sound familiar?

(The similarities don't stop there. Curiously enough, the singer, known for his tender evocations of childhood innocence, inveighs in his album *Foreigner* against all forms of phoniness: "phony mouth," "tears shed only in your eye," elders bringing up their children with "horns and holly-wooden songs, dead snakes and poisoned wisdoms between our teeth.")

I once toyed with the idea of writing an entire book of essays on the sub-ject of Cat Stevens, re-imagining him as the paradigmatic man of the late twentieth century. Why, you ask? (But, of course, you don't. You're not even reading this, but I'll answer you all the same.) Because: in his life and in his work, Stevens, the son of Greek and Swedish parents, jumped from the sphere of the individual to the sphere of the cosmic (perhaps you weren't keeping track, but the '70s were quite cosmic) all without having passed through what philosopher Ken Wilber claims is the necessary sphere of the tribal.

After World War II, we had all had enough of the tribal, yes? And the generations that followed avoided it at all costs, and who more so than a '70s pop star? Embodying this culturally imposed move, Stevens had nothing to sustain him in the sphere of the cosmic until ultimately he regressed, somewhat violently, back into the unlived tribal sphere, where he more or less remained for twice as many years as he'd spent in the public eye, running Islamic schools, raising money for Islamic charities, and endorsing (some say) the fatwah against Salman Rushdie, until recently when, having fully integrated the tribal, he has returned from it, attempting to reapproach the sphere of the universal, more or less, through it.

Or so it seems to me. Perhaps the royalties from his albums were simply beginning to lag.

In any case, Dear X, this is what concerns me about you: What, I wonder, is your famous retreat paradigmatic of?

Is it a highly principled reaction against the shallow corruptions and vapid demands of what in the '60s, when you left it, was still the literary market place, but which is now, for all practical purposes, nothing more than a withering branch of American entertainment culture? (As a child, I watched Mailer and Vidal and Capote on the *Dick Cavett* and *Merv Griffin* shows, their appearances simultaneously drawing attention to their books, while making them, in effect, obsolete.) How you must have shuddered at the thought of such mercantile buffoonery and its pandering! And now it's worse, with everyone and his dog on a book tour and Nobel Prize winners eating dinner with Oprah.

Is that what you turned your back on? Or does your self-withdrawal have to do with nothing more significant than good ole' fashioned American crankiness? Less Cat Stevens, say, and more Howard Hughes?

It matters, I think, because, at this point, the legend is threatening to over-whelm the work. (Were your face better known, surely it would appear alongside Marilyn's and Elvis's and James Dean's in that famous parody of Edward Hopper's *Nighthawks*.) Even *The Catcher in the Rye* has its dubious double life of American crankiness, accompanying assassins on their dark rounds.

Surely, this is not what you intended.

Is it too far-fetched, I'm wondering, to understand your withdrawal as an act of *imatio dei*, an imitation of God's *tzimtzum*, the kabbalistic move inward, essential for all creative work?

This is what I hope.

And I also hope that, one day, whatever work you have been doing for the last forty years will at last be published, and we will all come to understand that we were wrong to care about and pry into and quibble over a master's selfless insistence on maintaining the conditions his work required, work that has been and continues to be a gift to us all.

Dear Mr. Salinger,

I send my congratulations and my gratitude to you on this, the fiftieth anniversary of the publication of *The Catcher in the Rye*, a book that — despite everything — still matters.

> *Sincerely yours,*
> *Joseph Skibell*

❧ Joseph Skibell's debut novel, A *Blessing on the Moon,* won the Richard and Hinda Rosenthal Award from the American Academy of Arts and Letters. He teaches at Emory University.

Dear Mr. Salinger,

Since being named by my mother after the character in your story, I have often wondered how you intended its pronunciation, and from where you originally heard the name.

Though almost a case of "The Boy Named Sue," and it being more than a slight reason for the amusement of my peers, I wouldn't change it for the world now, even if I do get occasionally irritated by repetitively explaining its origin to the extent that concerns me and from where I received it.

Nonetheless, I am curious to probe deeper, and to follow the links back. As far as my naming goes, the story ends at your character, Zooey Glass, who I feel almost related to, yet I know not from where he sprang.

On another note, my family has always pronounced the name "Zo-E" yet I cannot help but feel that the intended pronunciation was "Zoo-E." I would be more than truly gratified if you could shed a little light on this for me.

Yours respectfully,
Zooey Ball

❦ Zooey Ball is a poet living in Cheltenham, England.

Dear Mr. Salinger,

I'd like to believe you're actually going to read this, but you're kind of like a distant galaxy, and all of us in this volume are little bleeps and pictures on some *Voyager*-like spacecraft. I mean, I'd like to think you're out there somewhere. I'd like to think you might someday make contact with us, feeble-yet-always-hopeful humanity. I also think of you as the Howard Hughes of literature. Do you grow your fingernails long? What is the movie you watch obsessively in your haven? Not *Ice Station Zebra*, Hughes's favorite, but maybe *Giant. Rebel without a Cause* would be too obvious . . . overrated in my estimation, anyway. Holden Caulfield has much more staying power as a rebel.

I suppose I sound disrespectful, my tone a little cheeky, but it would make a huge difference if I knew you were going to read this. Look, if you do, there is something I want to tell you . . . give me a call at 360-650-0403. I won't tell anyone. I promise.

That probably doesn't hold much weight with you, does it? My promise. I mean, people have broken your confidence before, right? There was Joyce Maynard. And I heard about some high school student who interviewed you once, or something like that. That must not have made your day, that Maynard book.

Okay, maybe I'd just tell my close family and my best friends. Maybe I'd only tell . . . the entire world. J. D. Salinger called me up! Can you believe it? Yeah, he said that of all the letters in the book, mine was the one that touched him the most, that brought a tear to his eye. It would be like some call from the president. Hey, that's an idea! You could be the president of the literary world! After someone writes a particularly noteworthy book or risks their literary reputation on a dangerous mission, you can give them a call to congratulate them the way the president does. Would you like that? Probably not.

I hear you've been writing away all these years, that after you die we're going to be deluged with J. D. Salinger manuscripts, that they're in some vault or something. I used to imagine manuscripts stacked up to the ceiling, you counting your pages like some miser counting loose change. What else do you have to do with your day? But what good is it keeping your stories to yourself? I used to think they probably couldn't be any good because you must be so out of touch with the rest of the world. But maybe you're not. I think you watch a lot of TV. So do I. I bet you bought one of those George Foreman grills off the TV, didn't you? So did I. You see, we have that in common. I feel such a connection.

Nine Stories is about my favorite story collection in the world. Really. I'm not just spouting off. I read "The Laughing Man" to my classes all the time. That's okay, isn't it? I mean, you're not going to sue me or anything. That drives me nuts, Jerry (you don't mind if I call you Jerry, do you?). I mean, people just want to be close to you because . . . it's your fault anyway. If you hadn't written in such a universally appealing way, we wouldn't think we all know you so well. But now it's too late and all you keep doing is suing or threatening to sue. That's how you show your gratitude?

Or, whoa, I didn't even think about this. Maybe you actually don't like anything you've written — maybe it's just self-doubt that's made you so reclusive. Maybe it's one of those self-loathing issues and that's why you don't want to have anything to do with the rest of us, because you loathe us all the more for loving you. Is that it? I hope not, but if you ever want to talk about it, you know where to reach me.

> *Your buddy,*
> *Robin Hemley*

🦋 Robin Hemley is the author of five books of fiction and nonfiction including *Turning Life into Fiction* and *The Last Studebaker*. He teaches creative writing at the University of Utah.

Dear J. D. Salinger,

Herewith a few words of encouragement and gratitude from a thirty-five-year-old Norwegian cartoonist who finds himself returning to your fine books regularly like old, reliable friends. To use Holden Caulfield's criteria, you're definitely an author I would want to call up on the phone (only, of course, you would possibly be the least willing person in the world to accept such a call; therefore this letter, whether you want it or not). Many have thoroughly analyzed your work. For my part I try to be one "who just reads and runs." But I would like to thank you for the exceptional intelligence, humanity, warmth, and humor of your works. Alas, these elements far too seldom go together in artistic expression. I believe that the comedic aspects of your work, especially, have been too often overlooked in deference to its perceived difficulties and "eccentricities." American humor from approximately 1910 to 1960 is one of the major joys in my life, and had I the opportunity to edit an anthology of its many riches, I would include not only the obligatory (and wonderful) Lardner, Marquis, Benchley, Thurber, Perelman, Bob and Ray, et al., but would also hope to include, for example, "Just Before the War with the Eskimos" and/or *Raise High the Roof Beam, Carpenters* — two comic masterpieces, among their other virtues. And if a writer wanted to learn how to be profoundly moving without becoming mawkish, he or she would do well to study the scene where Holden's little sister asks him to name just one thing that interests him. Thanks, also, for your integrity, in so many senses of the word. Hoping this finds you well, I remain,

Your friendly reader,
Waldemar Hepstein

P.S. I know the sound of one hand clapping. Unfortunately, this sound cannot be described in words.

❧   Waldemar Hepstein is a comic book artist, writer, and translator living in Oslo, Norway.

Eh, Monsieur:

Please excuse the impertinence of this letter and let me apologize for the impertinence of all the other writers herein. Although they may not say it, I will. We are not writing these letters to you. Indeed, we are merely writing to ourselves or to the part of ourselves that once had true literary aspirations, had honor, had good-hearted and honest artistic intentions, and was not jaded. I am sure you know the favorite vice of writers is masturbation. Beyond that, too many writers love to talk about writing. No wonder the young people of this country have retreated to television and computers. I swear to Christ there is nothing more boring than hearing writers wax on about literature and their own pissy contributions to it. What's even worse is to listen to writers who claim to understand the big picture of books, yet are unable to write a simple, engaging, whiskey-belching American sentence. Were we lucky enough to have the fame and money God bestowed on you, we would not waste our time with such crap as this exercise.

Frankly, I can't recall much of your writings, except of course that big novel that made you huge money and allowed you to run from the scheming, conniving, petulant world that is American literature, but I couldn't tell you the plot, the only thing that sticks in my mind is the business of "prostitute writers." But hey, I guess that's what we all are or aspire to be. The guys who hit the big time are whores or eventually get turned out as whores, but the lesser guys like me are surely sluts. But even those minor league poets like myself can break out of the penitentiary of iambic pentameter and become flash-in-the-pan whores. I have recently sold a novel to Hollywood and they are now filming it. Finally, I have become a "prostitute writer"! I only hope it brings me enough greenbacks to never have to write again, to never have to talk to another agent, editor, publisher, poetaster, or journalist. I hope I never have to send my obscure work to yet another obscure publication or university-sponsored literary journal. I hope to never have to stand in a bookstore and read the drippings of my heart to a scant and strangely longing crowd of American losers. I hope to never have to stand in front of a class full of freshman comp students who don't understand why a dependent clause should be set off by a comma. In short, I hope this stupid movie allows me to toss my computer out the window for evermore. Thank God literature is dying. It is dying, isn't it?

At any rate, here's to you, pal. Honestly, I don't even know if you're still living. Last I heard you were in New England banging young girls. I lived in New England for some years so I can't blame you. But, if it's true, more power to you. If it's not true, get some Viagra. But never mind, like I said, this letter is not to you. And, it's not really to me either. It's to Maurice Moyle, my high school English teacher in Yerington, Nevada. The year was 1962. That was the year they moved me from fullback to pulling guard. The state of Nevada was in a time warp. We had never even heard of Jack Kerouac who is far more important than you. We still ran the ridiculous single wing although more learned areas of the country ran the T or split-T. Mr. Moyle made us read your friggin' book. We all liked it because it spoke to us young folks. Moyle was a half-breed Paiute Indian like myself. I don't even know if he's still alive. He had a charcoal gray mohair sports coat, wore thin ties, and had coal-black eyes that told you he could kick your ass if he had to. He's the guy that made me love literature, and I know we spent a full week on *The Catcher in The Rye*, but I don't know if we said anything meaningful or even truly understood it.

Then again, what is meaningful to a teenager? Even though we can read great works as a teenager, all things eventually dissolve into meaninglessness. Sometimes I have a hard time recalling the first piece of tail that I ever got. I'm fairly sure it was in a cathouse since cathouses were and are legal in most of Nevada. I couldn't tell you what the woman looked like or if I enjoyed it. It was just a rite of passage for us hicks in the sticks of the high, western desert. I have lost that true memory. It doesn't matter. We are born lost, only to gain a little bit of wisdom and then watch our bodies disintegrate almost at that same time we begin to gain that true insight into this cheap puzzle of life. Imagine the descendants of the Ghost Dance messiah Wovoka reading your book in the small desert valley of so long ago. . . . Anyway, to make a long story short, this Bud's for you. And it's for me too. But, it's especially for my high school English teacher. Au revoir, my man. Don't take any wooden nickels! Especially beware of those Indian head nickels. Thanks, I think, for encouraging me in this peculiar direction.

Sincerely,
Adrian C. Louis

❦   Adrian C. Louis is a member of the Lovelock Paiute Indian Tribe and is the author of ten poetry and short story collections. He teaches at Southwest State University in Minnesota.

Dear Jerry,

Look. I appreciate your predicament. No one has been more sympathetic to your situation as I have. But I told you not to take in that little Yale strumpet, didn't I? Sure we all get a little woozy when we see the occasional coed on the cover of the *Times* magazine. But that one looked like trouble from the get-go. Of course she was going to publish a memoir. Christ, your mailman probably has a development deal with Miramax. And yes, your own daughter came out with her version. Well, I didn't read her book (did anyone?). And now Matt acting in movies. I feel your pain.

Still, Jerry, I hope you realize the irony in your complaining about people exploiting your life when you consider what you've done to mine. And stop trying to soft-sell it. How do I put this?

Could you please leave us alone! The wildflowers, the soybean chocolates, the wheat germ recipes, the pages.

The pages and pages and pages. I just don't have the time. I have my own life. So has Phoebe. First it was the "Seymour Saga" — "Seymour: A Prologue," "Seymour: An Appendix," "Seymour: An Index." To quote that little old lady in the hamburger commercial: "Where's the beef?" You know, the middle bit?

Okay, so the beef, the middle bit, came soon enough. That box of Glass. But 3,916 pages! Remember that picture of Max Perkins with his foot on that crate spilling over with manuscript, that exquisite literary bile of Thomas Wolfe? Remember that?

I have that foot! I have that box! Jerry, your cup runneth over, and it's flooding my apartment. I understand your wanting my opinion before you send it over to Little, Brown or the *New Yorker*.

But since little Fran was born (we call her Fran-2), things have been a little hectic around here. And to tell you the truth, we're all a bit "Salingered out" at the moment. Sure, some of the Glass saga is great stuff. The Boo-

Boo deep-sea fishing episode. Zooey's ice cream shop ("The Zen Cone" — very good). But seventeen pages on Waker's Matchbox toy car collection? Nine odes to Seymour's thumbs? I'm sure thems is great digits, Jerry, but could that perchance be a tad much? Likewise, the rhapsodic paean to the taste of Walt's sweat. Like, whatever.

Yeah, I got through as much of it as I could. Phoebe had more problems than I did. She's a little put out by the myriad inaccuracies. She's also, to tell you the truth, not a little disappointed that you've decided to continue using the name "Glass." It is, as you can't fail to notice, perhaps a little too close to "Glash."

When I married into the wonderfully eccentric Glash clan, I had no idea they were the models for your celebrated "fictional" Glass stories. People marveled (as I did, as an undergraduate at Brown) at the beautifully rendered details of the supposedly created "universe" of this fabricated family. Phoebe, of course, saw it differently, and to be honest, she's sorry that fate brought the Glashes and Salingers together in the same apartment building before the war.

But she's been decent about it, even when you took what she said was her mother Francine's "minor existential crisis" and blew it up into that long, tortured story in the *New Yorker*. That was when her mom was forced to stop calling herself "Franny" and had to resort to the more severe "Francine" (a name she always hated) in an attempt to obscure the connection. (Even now, all these years later, people still ask me if my mother-in-law is *that* Franny.)

So, you asked me if you should publish *The Glass Family Chronicles* (bad title!). And although it pains me to say so — because I know you've been working on this for almost fifty years now — I have to say no. In fact, if you attempt to turn any of this material public, I'm afraid that on behalf of Franny, Zooey, Walter, Waker and all the members of the vast Glash brood, I'll be forced to employ the services of Blitzberg, Doltz and Kline. In case you're wondering, they're the guys who stopped Thomas Pynchon from publishing his seven-volume *Greenberg Saga* (which would have violated the privacy of a very nice, quiet family who live on Riverside and 72nd), and they also helped Truman Capote dismantle most of "Answered Prayers."

Answer my prayers, Jerry — throw the stuff in the river. If you want to do something constructive, open up a health-food restaurant in Cornish, NH. Fran always said you were a good cook.

Sincerely,
J. B. Miller

❧   J. B. Miller is a writer living in New York. His plays include *White Lies* and *Shirkers*. He is also a regular contributor to Salon.com.

Dear Mr. Salinger —

Some years ago, actually in the summer issue of the *Paris Review*, 1981, we published an account of a curious interview with you conducted by one Betty Eppes, a young part-time tennis professional, who was a Special Assignments Editor for the "Fun" section of both the Baton Rouge *Advocate* and *State Times*. In the spring of the previous year she had persuaded her managing editor (much against his better judgment) to let her spend her summer vacation trying to interview you. She flew to Boston, rented a sky-blue Pinto, and drove into the Green Mountains to Windsor, which is the nearest place to Cornish which has lodgings. She wrote you a letter which she left with the Windsor post office, knowing you would get it. In it she said she was a budding novelist, needed some advice, a great admirer, of course, that she was tall with green eyes and red-gold hair, and that at 9:30 the next morning she would wait by the covered bridge in her sky-blue Pinto for thirty minutes before heading back to Louisiana.

You may remember that something in her letter touched you in some way — the effort she'd gone through, the green eyes and red-gold hair or whatever — and that you'd gone down over the river to see her. You leaned in the car window and she had time for seven or eight questions ("Did you consciously opt for a writing career, or did you just drift into it?") before you realized she was actually a reporter on the prowl and abruptly you turned back for the covered bridge.

In the process of preparing our lengthy account of her trip (including your increasingly peremptory answers) Ms. Eppes told us that eleven days after her story was published, you sent her care of the *Advocate* photostats of an order blank you had sent away to New York. In it you asked for two over-sized schoolbags, gift-wrapped from Denmark (at $16.50 each) that had been advertised in the then current *New Yorker*.

Ms. Eppes told us that she had been driven "just about crazy" trying to figure out why you would send her such a thing. We too are intrigued. Is there some hidden meaning here? Why a "Danish" schoolbag? Why is the letter dated five years earlier? Is there some significance to "over-sized"? Does the Chocolate Soup address (there is no such place today) suggest that Zimbabwe is somehow involved in the Glass family history? Is the number 10003 a clue of some kind?

In sum, Mr. Salinger, much to be considered, and I hope you will take the time to do so.

Sincerely yours,
George Plimpton

🦋 George Plimpton is an author, humorist, actor, and American icon. He edits the *Paris Review.*

Dear Mr. Salinger,

Before I pick a bone with you — a small one, really, itsy-bitsy — I want, as I suspect a zillion others do, to thank you for, among other things, teaching me to smoke. Well, to be less coy, teaching me how to use smoking — the lighting up, the putting out, the in- and exhaling — as a device for pacing scene, as well as for revealing character. In addition, I want to thank you for teaching me generosity, for my Fat Lady as well as for all others I've yet to meet. Thanks, too, for making "phony" a necessary word in my vocabulary, and making your Huck miss all those folks, bent and straight, the world is made of. Thanks, yes, for all those Glass kids — precocious, vulnerable, poetic and undaunted — and for putting before us the model for all those girls with "house counting" eyes. Thanks for tall tales and the tall tellers at the front of the bus. Thanks for that half of sandwich and the war we won't be fighting with the Eskimos. Thanks for the new definition for "kike," and for nuns at art school. Thanks, in brief, for all those stories that have become metaphors impossible to live without.

The bone? Lordy, it's this: Why did you permit Seymour to kill himself? So what if he's married, no matter the year or the condition of her finger nails, to a Spiritual Tramp? So what if a stranger or two has a nose slathered with zinc oxide? So what if young people have the annoying habit of teasing (what are probably annoying) dogs? So what if one's feet become the subject of some interest in an elevator? You see, by letting Seymour blow his brains all over room 507 at the end of "A Perfect Day for Bananafish," you gave every generation thereafter of would-be writers a far too convenient way to end every story. Literally, a license to kill. The world is too much with you? Well, Bunky, put a noose around the neck. Surrounded by numbskulls and taskmasters? Get in the car, close the garage door, turn on the engine, turn the radio to the channel that plays "Oh, Lonesome Me." Neighbors can't appreciate your garden of nightshade and kudzu? Get thee to Lover's Leap. Spouse unwilling to pack bags for spur of the moment trip to Timbuktu? Put your lawn chair down in the passing lane of I-95. See, Mr. Salinger, every young writer, having been moved by the magic you made between margins, now sees such to be the only, if not the inevitable, solution to the pickles that stories put characters in. Such a "move" has become the first thing the *deus* does when he hops out of the *machina*. What's worse, the more "unreasonable" and evidently "unmotivated" the move, whether by pill or pistol or paper bag, the more, er, artsy-fartsy the moment, the more we readers are supposed to gasp at the profundity of yet another tender-hearted protagonist opening up his or her arms to greet the outer darkness. Seymour, of course, has become an analogue for every young writer who imagines himself too smart, too sensitive and too spiritual for this vale of etceteras. And, sheesh, these writers, as innocent of craft as they seem to be of real life, are killing heroes off at a spookily fast pace. (Henry James, you'll remember, had something of the same problem; see Miss Daisy Miller for the full explanation.) Me, I'm wondering what you'd do now to end that less than perfect day. Maybe that's what you're working on at present — an apology for the "slight" exaggeration, say, Buddy made telling the story the first time around. Maybe we are to hear from Seymour himself on the subject? C'mon, tell us the Ortgies 7.65 automatic jammed and that our hero himself makes a call, collect, to someone in Whirly Wood to say, by golly, life ain't so bad after all.

Remember, though, that my "complaint" is small, no more than a trifle, for it's all the other moves, each meet and indispensable, that I'm typing to say "yippee" for, from the corner at which we're to meet the ones we love and the watches we are to send to the empty pools we're to stumble into and the desperate phone calls we make to tell our horrible lies. Yes, it is another "exquisite" day here at the border of China and Paris, France, and all of us in the hinterlands, Mickey Mickeranno and Jimmy Jimmereeno included, are gathered on the Sports Deck eager to hear another yarn about us free of "logic and intellectual stuff."

Blessings,
Lee K. Abbott

❧   Lee K. Abbott has published six collections of fiction including *Wet Places at Noon*. He is the director of the MFA program in creative writing at Ohio State University.

Dear J. D. Salinger,

My weakness for the high drama of small consolations goads me sometimes to gaze on the beauties of punctuation, but especially on your deli-
cately sumptuous use of the parenthesis throughout the monologue of
your 1959 novella, *Seymour: An Introduction.*

I've even counted them. Your parentheses rise everywhere from this aus-
terely garrulous fiction, paired in a volume with *Raise High the Roof
Beam, Carpenters.* On 75 percent of the pages in *Seymour,* parentheses
nip at the surrounding sentences, or swell to meet them. They help to give
Buddy Glass, your first-person narrator, his self and his freedom. Parentheses also allow a rhythmic spirituality to adulterate the body of prose.

Let's not neglect, while we're at it, the frequent use of em dashes in
Buddy's slapstick reverie, your novella, which he claims to be composing
as the introduction (please note your title) for a posthumous edition of
Seymour's poetry. Buddy — himself a writer — is Seymour's younger
brother. He extols the late poet and the poetry in fond, long verbal waves
and combers. Your nervy dashes nick the waters like fizzing ocean white-
caps. Very resourceful.

But dashes are somehow just more flexible. Habitually we think in convenient fast fragments pierced by their sleek, short spears. So dashes are
easily coaxed into paragraphs. Parentheses, no.

Few writers make the effort to orchestrate parens, to use them anew.
Almost no one puts them to work while also playing with them. But
you do.

I wonder if parentheses can be considered as the refuge for a mind.
Sometimes I want to rest in them. You urge me to.

For example.

(For example.)

Doesn't the second version, dangling above, beckon to us better, improving on the first with the addition of sinuous curved borders? Even without benefit of much true content, parens hold on to something, keep it safe. There we can stay, too. They are ethical, conserving the observed, and they are helplessly aesthetic, luring the mind's eye. (I'm reminded of a gift of brandied plums afloat in a wily glass jar. For years I kept both plums and jar, moving them with me from home to home. The cook had sugared and strained an idea that I couldn't quite understand. I needed more time.)

Mr. Salinger, nudged by your parens into whims of my own, I swerve toward plums only because I'm obeying your tongue.

But I also wish to explain why parentheses in *Seymour* seize my attention.

Your parentheses seem meant to relax time and slow it down, even when they click nervously. When I see them before I read them, at first they seem to quiver and regret; yet as I read on, they settle, and so do I. They're unconventionally steadying. Or, as Buddy puts it, a few pages into the story:

> I'm aware that a good many perfectly intelligent people can't stand parenthetical comments while a story's purportedly being told. . . . I'm here to advise that not only will my asides run rampant from this point on (I'm not sure, in fact, that there won't be a footnote or two) but I fully intend, from time to time, to jump up personally on the reader's back when I see something off the beaten plot line that looks exciting or interesting and worth steering toward.

Parentheses offer Buddy a way to move more completely as a brother and a writer around his subject (Seymour) and around his reader: up and sideways and excitedly, without stopping steering. But he doesn't have to hurry, and he certainly doesn't have to bushwhack a straight path. Parens usher him on, whatever his misgivings. They don't shove, though. Parens allow him to "run rampant," as if converting faux pas into footsteps. They prevent him from knowing or deciding sooner than he should. *Where to?* For him, the question *is* the answer. Thanks to parens, he sidles around unexpected corners.

Parens safeguard paradox for Buddy without interrupting the momentum of the pages. They contain a contrary idea without squeezing or betraying it. Outside, the prevailing forces will not invade. In this way, Buddy's ambivalence about almost everything finds an arena to thrive in.

Rhythm has been mentioned before, but I should say it again: Parens, whether confined or flowing, make the difference between prose that dances and words that only tell, tell, tell. Like prayer, denunciation, revelation, or poetry, your writing *shows* what it is: the hopping soul of Buddy, landing briefly.

Your parens also supply Buddy with a good place for his extremism to steep a while. They let him linger on the odd thought without being chased away by it. The solitude of a writer lost in contemplation may chafe at the ear; on a bad day, lonesomeness savages our scruples. Parentheses help stave off the damage. Because of parens, Buddy can seclude himself and not suffer the consequences.

It might be interesting to consider why you don't use even more parentheses, given their attractions. Would it have been pragmatic to include three or four times the number you have in *Seymour?*

The notion gives me pause. My eye begins to wander.

One possible effect of parentheses in the overwhelming plural: the look and feel of a speckled secrecy. With far more of them, the page would shift around aurally like a warren of whispers. Not right, since Buddy is pure candour. Besides, all the muttering could interrupt the main action.

Which raises the question: What is *Seymour's* main action?

It is the sound of someone speaking — alone.

Parentheses make solitude a little more habitable. (For all concerned.)

With best wishes,
Molly McQuade

🦋   Molly McQuade is a poet living in Maryland. Her first book was called *An Unsentimental Education.* She has also been a fellow of the New York Foundation for the Arts.

Dear Mr. Salinger:

Some forty years ago, along with David Lloyd Stevenson, I was preparing an anthology that was published under the title, *Stories of Modern America*. We requested permission from you to reprint one of your stories. You wrote a short note to deny us the privilege. Alas, your note seems to have disappeared; in those days I didn't save letters, having Thoreau as my model and trying to live an unencumbered life.

But the mysterious last sentence of your note is fixed in my memory. It read: "I have my reasons."

Later in the sixties, I wrote an essay about San Francisco for the magazine *Holiday*, which engaged Arnold Newman to do a group photograph of San Francisco writers. One of those invited to appear in a café before the camera was the beatnik-hippie poet and prosateur Richard Brautigan. I explained the situation to him. He considered. He refused to appear, saying, "I have my reasons."

I was powerfully struck by these two very different writers uttering refusals with the identical words. Fortunately, I knew Brautigan well enough to ask why he would not appear; he was often photographed, even for book jackets, with enigmatically unidentified young women, usually with long hair in the fashion of that blessed era.

He explained that he wanted to be photographed alone, with no other writers in the frame.

So, dear admired J. D. Salinger, please follow the logic here: Did your rejection of our offer mean that you wanted your story to be the only one in the anthology? Or was there another reason, too delicate to be uttered at that time, which you could now share with the ghost of David Lloyd Stevenson and the undersigned?

I would be most grateful. I too have reasons.

>   *Sincerely yours,*
>   *Herbert Gold*

❧   Herbert Gold is the author of many books including the novels *Fathers* and A *Girl of Forty.* He lives in San Francisco, California.

Dear J. D. Salinger,

I have searched for clues to your disappearance. When I first read *The Catcher in the Rye* and *Franny and Zooey* as a teenager, you had already stopped publishing more than three decades before. I figured you were dead. The fictional worlds you painted — your descriptions of youthful angst over society's falseness and pressure to conform — were so harsh and tactile to me. I had come of age *after* a social era meant to vanquish, or at least expose, the hypocrisy of the gray-flannel elite. But you, who as I learned were much alive, missed taking part in even that social upheaval. You know, it didn't really seem to work much anyway.

Still, I can't help but wonder why, for so many years, you've decided to play your music in the closet of your own making, leaving the rest of the world increasingly deaf. Does it have something to do with the fact that the collective American hearing is damaged, even more so today, by the annoying mantra "You've got mail" or the opening bells of the New York Stock Exchange? (I don't know, maybe you've invested well all these years. I've never read an interview, however, with J. D. Salinger's broker.)

I know the cacophony of pop culture is wearing. It's a worldwide disease born here in this country. Even the mumble of the Jesus Prayer would seem to be better background noise for the anguished, cranky existence so many people feel, but have no idea how to describe in words.

Recently, I reread the two books and looked again for answers. As anyone can see, you don't owe any one of us anything, especially when the phony bastards have only multiplied in all these decades. (A faculty member I know recently termed the tenor of the Ivory Tower exchange: "elegant pettiness.")

But I can't help but mourn anyway. When Holden Caulfield and Franny became depressed for the right reasons — false loves and sanctioned bullies, cocktail party prattling and adults with thick, gray-wool minds — they also came back for the right reasons. Sure, we never knew if they sold out

35

or fashioned their own, truly alternative paths. The selling-out idea seems doubtful, and we can only hope modern society wouldn't have swallowed their souls and given their descendants SUVs to drive. And of course I can, at least, visit them again and again and hear them speak as they still do to me, and as they hopefully will to my own children some day.

In the end, I guess you, like Holden, decided not to ever tell anybody anything again. But, even so, don't you miss everybody?

    Sincerely,
    Joanne Cavanaugh Simpson

Joanne Cavanaugh Simpson is a journalist and lecturer at Johns Hopkins University's Writing Seminars and Part-Time Graduate Program. Her articles have appeared in the *Miami Herald,* the *Baltimore Sun,* and *American Journalism Review.*

Dear Mr. Salinger,

In an essay in *Mystery and Manners*, Flannery O'Connor says that James Jones, whose work she deplored, claimed Thomas Wolfe as his inspiration. She goes on to say that when he wrote his books, Wolfe must have had no inkling of the damage for which he would be responsible. Composing the pieces that make up *Nine Stories*, you probably had no inkling of the damage for which you would be responsible, and my own stories are some of it. I read *Nine* when I was about nineteen — an age when reading can be an at least mildly dangerous activity. Actually, "For Esmé — with Love and Squalor" was my first encounter with your work; it was in *Fifty Great Short Stories*, a text for my first year English class at U. Va., and "For Esmé" remains, in my view, your ultimate writing — and maybe the ultimate, all-time short story. I suspect myself of continually trying to write my version of it. I'm incorrigible, no more likely to stop trying than I am to succeed. From where I sit (pecking away at my keyboard), this is not such a bad thing. It gives me, as they say in sports, something to shoot for. From where you sit, it must be dreadful. If you ever read anything of mine, you'll probably be cringing in recognition of my imitation and thievery of various aspects of your work. I'm inordinately fond of certain Salinger sentences. So I suppose this occasion is one where I can apologize to you for all the damage I've done in the name of being inspired by your writing. I'd also like to thank you for the many years of pleasure your work has given me — I'm especially grateful that your stories always stand up to my desire to be taught and delighted. I can read them again and again without disappointment. Finally, I must warn you: should you run across a story of mine in some journal that makes its way to your house, don't read it. It'll just irk you.

My very best to you,
David Huddle

🦋 David Huddle is a widely published poet and fiction writer. He teaches creative writing at the University of Vermont and at the Bread Loaf School of English.

Dear J. D. Salinger,

In 1993, when my first fiction appeared in print, it was my great good fortune that my debut was in the pages of the *New Yorker*. Dan Menaker, the editor who plucked my pages from the slush pile, told me that some of the *New Yorker* fiction staff had deemed my story "Salingerian." It occurred to me then — one of the many thrills connected with that heady moment of publication — that you might actually read it, if in fact you still read the *New Yorker*. (This was in the very earliest of Tina Brown's days.)

I have never studied writing formally, have no degree of any kind, and my mentors have no idea that I exist. You are one such mentor, so when my first novel was published two years later, in 1995, I sent you one of the first six finished copies I received, inscribed "To J. D. Salinger with great admiration from Katharine Weber."

A month later, the parcel was in my mailbox, stamped REFUSED. Ever since then, it has sat on a high shelf in my study, a constant rebuke to me from you. How dare I send you my first novel with its presumptuous inscription! Who did I think I was? Who did I think you were?

Katharine Weber

❧   Katharine Weber is the author of the novels *Objects in Mirror Are Closer Than They Appear* and *The Music Lesson*. She teaches fiction writing at Yale.

Dear Mr. Salinger:

In a really horrible review of my new book of stories, *Big Bend*, the woman writing says that the first story in the book is pretty good (thanks a lot, lady) but is "hampered by the presence of an unnaturally empathetic woman-child, like a cousin of a J. D. Salinger creation." The reviewer clearly means this as an insult, but of course it's a grand compliment: I have been compared to you. And the comparison is unnaturally empathetic, since I have learned everything from you about how natural a child's empathy and sympathy is, and how powerful youth and how fully formed every child and every teen is, insane programs to reach them (break them) notwithstanding. *The Catcher in The Rye* and I are both almost fifty, and that amazing book found me when I was twelve. You made it possible for me to be a teen then, to know I was right about at least one thing: adults are just as fucked as kids. And then the *Nine Stories*. Oh, Lord, Bananafish and all, stories I was in no way sure I understood, and yet read over and over and carried around and carried to college and quoted to girls and started my writing in imitation of.

So thanks for that, and thanks for disappearing, the only sane second act for any writer ever. Me, I've just quit my tenured job at Ohio State and have returned to Maine (where I belong), back home to write and be an unnaturally empathetic kid again, where I can only hope to be some kind of cousin to you, sir.

> *With love and respect,*
> *Bill Roorbach*

❦   Bill Roorbach is the author of five books, including a Flannery O'Connor Award–winning collection of stories, *Big Bend*, and a new novel, *The Smallest Color*.

Mr. Salinger,

Your mailbox must be a repository for deferred dreams — full of letters re-sembling children's appeals to presidential pets or holiday mascots. I imag-ine a generation of the culture-drunk, aware in their own ignorant way, picturing you something like this: a combination of James Earl Jones and Sean Connery, you sit at a simple wood desk in a steel shed in the forest, Styrofoam cooler of frozen peas at your side. You pound away on an old typewriter and slip finished chapters about the Glass family into a fire-proof drop-safe with no known combination. Zen and Hindi spirits congregate just outside, smoking, squinting, spitting. Who wouldn't wish on that image? Let me throw my quarter into that fountain — make me a real writer!

As a young, half-baked literary type I wrote a baggy, autobiographical jumble that I called a novel. The work had one coherent aspect: an epigram from *Seymour: An Introduction*: "Seymour once said all we do our whole lives is go from one little piece of Holy Ground to the next." The book was bad, but the life was good — fervid and riddled with new faiths. We had some fine times in the park, on the sidewalks, trailing through the used bookstores — me, you, Zooey, Teddy, Lane, the short man with the cigar in *Raise High the Roof Beam, Carpenters*. I believed then in what Seymour said. I still do.

You don't have to publish. You don't have to read the letters or reviews. You don't have to explain. We've got what we need. Don't say another word. But, for your sake, I hope you're still on Holy Ground, and I hope you're laughing. You better be able to laugh at that caricature of the Man in the Shed. Because it's a caricature of us, not you. Though ultimately there isn't any difference.

> *Sincerely,*
> *Andy Selsberg*

🦋 Andy Selsberg was a staff writer for the *Onion* and received an MFA in fiction writing from Brown University. He is working on a collection of stories.

Dear Mr. Salinger,

Sometimes the best advice about writing comes on shirt cardboard. In *Seymour: An Introduction*, Buddy Glass rereads old notes from his late brother about Buddy's fiction, jotted on shirt cardboard and scraps of paper. One note in particular expresses Seymour's irritation at one of Buddy's opening lines: "Henshaw woke up that morning with a splitting head." As Seymour writes to his brother, "I count so heavily on you to finish off all the fraudulent Henshaws in fiction. There just are no Henshaws."

Seymour's advice is my yardstick for determining authenticity in fiction. Whenever I read or write a line that forces a character into a situation, I dub it "a Henshaw" and quit reading or writing that particular piece. The worst thing a writer can do to a character is relegate him or her to a situation in which there can be no surprises.

Like few guides to writing except for Rilke's *Letters to a Young Poet*, *Seymour: An Introduction* offers humane but unsentimental advice to aspiring writers. In Seymour's forthright notes to Buddy, Seymour shows that subject, voice and character can't be separated from a story as clinical, disparate elements, but must be part of a whole product that reveals the inconsistencies of his (Buddy's) own heart. (Sorry if I've mangled Faulkner a bit.) Similarly, when Holden Caulfield speaks bitterly of phonies, when he attempts to scratch out the word "Fuck" on the school wall, he's trying to shield kids from learning to talk in an empty way. Henshaw is as removed from human emotions as his name — not so unlike Holden at times, but without the redeeming vulnerability. Holden is an expert at detecting phonies because he has tried on some pretensions himself and failed, though with wit and charm. So when we read about Henshaw waking with a splitting headache, the same engaging quirkiness isn't there.

Instead of engaging our sympathy or curiosity, each throb of Henshaw's headache becomes ours.

Carolyn Alessio

🦋   Carolyn Alessio is a writer who teaches at Cristo Rey High School in Chicago, Illinois. She also edits prose for *Crab Orchard Review*.

Dear Mr. Salinger —

I should like this letter to be extremely squalid and moving, but I will be grateful if at the very least it expresses my admiration for and appreciation of your work, especially *Nine Stories*.

"For Esmé — with Love and Squalor" was one I didn't read right away, probably because I didn't identify, immediately, with the maleness and militariness of the narrator. And you'll concede that the plot doesn't tickle the same titillation feathers as "Bananafish" or "Teddy."

But the ending of "Esmé" is shocking in its own way, and it occurs to me that this is perhaps because of what happens in those other stories. I love how you have Sergeant X step outside himself to narrate the exchange with Corporal Z, his reflection on the scribbled *cri de coeur* "Dear God, life is hell," and, ultimately, the redemption he finds in the orphan Esmé's note and the gift of her dead father's wristwatch. Because we've been hearing the story in the third-person voice, the switch back to first — in the final paragraph — makes his salvation all the sweeter, and closer to home. Call me corny, but it warms my h-e-a-r-t every time.

The voice in "Esmé" is, it seems, opposite to the one in "Bananafish," which keeps us outside Seymour's consciousness and calls on us to infer, from his own exchanges and from the phone conversation between the girl and her mother, glimpses into what his state of mind may be. Like most, I'll never forget reading the story for the first time and the effect of the last sentence. "Wait, wait, wait," I said to myself, "let me go back, I missed something." But that is, no doubt, exactly what the girl thinks in the wake of the suicide as the story continues beyond its ending on the page. I used to think it was unfair of you to cut off our acquaintance with Seymour in such a violent, abrupt way. Now I see how closely you were rendering the experience of real life; how my frustration mirrors that of anyone who has come to know someone over time, and lost that person suddenly, especially to his own hand.

Your *Nine Stories* contains more truth — more revelations — than any one book has a right to. I read them when I want to be reminded of the way people speak, and of the connections that lie, either in a potential or realized state, between seemingly unlikely souls (Seymour and Sybil, Esmé and Sergeant X, Ginnie and Franklin). We are all fortunate that you have never hesitated to display your acquaintance with squalor — and love,

Jessica Treadway

🦋 Jessica Treadway is the author of a short story collection, *Absent without Leave*, and a novel, *And Give You Peace*. She directs the MFA creative writing program at Emerson College in Boston.

Dear Mr. Salinger:

Forgive my impertinence. You've spent the bulk of your life, I know, ducking people like me, people eager to tell you how your work has changed our lives. That might not be so bad, but then we're all set to tell you *about* those lives, our tangled, wistful histories. Too often we've brought along a short story or two that you might want to look at. I imagine you crouched defensively before an endless stream of us, the needy and hopeful. And now along come these letters, just when it might have been safe to go outside.

So I'll keep this brief. I first read *The Catcher in the Rye* one Friday night when I was in high school. Saturday I read it again, and on Monday I went to the library for your other books. From the first I fell a little in love with the books' wit and their festooning sentences — a prose rhythm, as this sentence attests, that I carry still. But what kept me reading and rereading was the sense of relief, that at last I had found the work I had been trying to find. I read your books as if they were Scripture, and more than once to friends quoted this passage from *Seymour: An Introduction*:

> At a certain period of his life (usually, grievous to say, a *successful* period), a man may suddenly feel it Within His Power to confess that he cheated on his final exams in college, he may even choose to reveal that between the ages of twenty-two and twenty-four he was sexually impotent, but these gallant confessions in themselves are no guarantee that we'll find out whether he once got piqued at his pet hamster and stepped on its head.

Here's what I understand the passage, like most of your work, to be saying: Knock off the bushwah. Quit posturing. Do your work. And, characteristically, it is said with grace, strength, and a saving asperity. I was grateful to you for your clear vision then, and I still am.

Sincerely,
Erin McGraw

❧ Erin McGraw is the author of two collections of stories, *Bodies at Sea* and *Lies of the Saints.* She teaches English at Ohio State University.

Dear Mr. Salinger,

You made the right decision. I've sometimes wished that I'd followed your example, although I'd have missed meeting hundreds of wonderful people.

As for that hack who won your confidence and then betrayed you, I'm certain that her karma reeks of weak ink, sour grape, and spilled bean.

Feel fine,
Tom Robbins

🦋 Tom Robbins is the author of seven novels, the most recent of which, *Fierce Invalids Home from Hot Climates*, won the Best Novel of 2000 award from the Audio Publishers Association. He has lived in and around Seattle since 1962.

Dear J. D. Salinger,

Just a note. No need for an answer.

I simply wanted to congratulate you on the way you've conducted your life. When Maynard's book happened I made a note in my journal that that whining vixenette got more press coverage than you have had in your entire career for your work. The interesting point here is that all of this has quickly vaporized but your work hasn't.

Very early in my late teens I was struck by the energy and strength of your intentions. How strongly you meant what you had to say. This is characteristic of the highest nature that fiction can assume, but is still rare indeed.

I also wanted to offer my admiration for your insistent privacy. This is the age of the writer as self-publicist and I can't quite see the possible benefits other than accumulated airline mileage that allows one an almost equal privacy in Marseille or Vera Cruz.

Meanwhile I hope you keep writing. Tu Fu, perhaps the greatest Chinese poet, published no books in his lifetime but did quite well afterwards.

> *Yours,*
> *Jim Harrison*

❧   Jim Harrison is a novelist and poet living in northern Michigan.

Dear Mr. Salinger,

Your example suggests that it is sufficient to say little.

Someone tells me he knows where you live, as if knowing this is a way of getting even: the revelation that will make you pay, at last, for the social sin of your relative silence.

His example suggests that neither Holden Caulfield nor anyone else can erase all of anything from the world. Innocence is its own reward, as is seclusion.

I sometimes imagine that you wrote to quiet your brain. If it seems undue conjecture to suggest that a prose writer of such precision and elemental revelation might have written to quiet his brain, well, I know something of the method. But I have reasons beyond my own practice to imagine it to be so.

Say this then: that to imagine what I have imagined about a writer is to suggest that a person who writes and publishes a little and then stops may be thought either to have said all he had to say or to have found words insufficient.

Perhaps few would liken you to Beckett, but it seems apt.

> *Sincerely,*
> *Marvin Bell*

❦ Marvin Bell lives in Iowa City, Iowa; Sag Harbor, New York; and Port Townsend, Washington. The latest of his seventeen books of poetry and essays is *Nightworks: Poems, 1962–2000.* He is the Flannery O'Connor Professor of Letters at the Iowa Writers' Workshop.

Dear Mr. Salinger,

Thank you for your books. When they asked me to be a part of this project I couldn't think of anything that more completely misunderstood the very clear messages of your books and your life, but here I am anyway to say thank you. Sorry.

I don't have any questions to ask you. They're all answered in the books. And I don't want more books. I don't want to know if you get up and go to your machine every day and worry about the people who are alive and about to do things on your pages. That's yours and they're yours, and no one should take that away from you, not after how hard you've worked to keep it.

Make sure you burn it all, that's my only warning. Maybe the house, too. That might sound nuts, but trust me.

Not to bring you down or anything.

Anyway, I hope this finds you well and reading something you love. Lately I've been more and more impressed with Alice Munro's stories.

> *Thanks again,*
> *Stewart O'Nan*

✤   Stewart O'Nan's award-winning fiction includes *Snow Angels*, *The Names of the Dead*, and *The Speed Queen*. In 1996, Granta named him one of the Best Young American Novelists.

This is to imperfectly and incompletely say my thanks, Mr. Salinger, for the serious, moving children and the seriously childlike adults who live in your fiction. Thank you, especially, for having given us "For Esmé — with Love and Squalor," which is one of the great war stories in all our literature — as great as (while so different from) Hemingway's "In Another Country" — and in no small measure because it takes place in what is alleged as (and shown to be) peacetime. It shows civilians as warriors and victims. It — and you, sir — taught us to risk emotion; to permit its very telling to be part of the story's action; to dare to love our characters out loud upon our pages; and to strive for clarity while respecting the mystery at the core of our characters, our readers, and ourselves.

With deepest gratitude,
Frederick Busch

🦋   Frederick Busch is the author of twenty-four books, the most recent of which are *Don't Tell Anyone: Short Stories and a Novella* and the novels *Girls* and *The Night Inspector.*

Dear Mr. Salinger,

I read *The Catcher in the Rye* when I was twelve. For the first time in my life, I couldn't turn pages fast enough. I read your short stories and *Franny and Zooey* when I was just out of college and starting an acting career (I didn't know that I'd write a couple of novels later in life).

What stays with me the most from your books is the Fat Lady from *Franny and Zooey*. I remember Seymour telling his siblings to polish their shoes for the fat lady who always came to see them and sat in the studio audience of their radio show. I remember Zooey explaining years later to Franny that there wasn't really a Fat Lady, that the Fat Lady is God, or that faceless, unknown person in the audience for whom a performer must always do his or her best, even when we don't feel like it, or when we're confronted with a cold, unresponsive, audience.

I can't tell you how many performances the Fat Lady has gotten me through. I remember a Broadway play I was in that had just opened and been thoroughly, unanimously, mercilessly trashed by every single New York critic. Since we didn't have the good fortune to close the play immediately, the actors had to go to the theatre and do a performance the next night. There are few things more painful for an actor than a second night on Broadway when the critics have bombed you. Audiences are hostile and don't want to be there. I got through the show that wintry night by reminding myself that the Fat Lady must be in the audience, that she'd come a long way and gone to a lot of trouble to get her ticket, and that she was, in fact, thrilled beyond measure to be seeing the play and therefore deserved the best I could give.

The Fat Lady has also inspired me through countless matinees in front of cold, mirthless audiences, or worse, subscription audiences for nonprofit theatres. I always tell myself that there's someone out there who's loving it, needing it, being nourished by it. And because of your book, I'm sure that's true. *Franny and Zooey* is God's, and your, gift to actors. For that I can never thank you enough.

Sincerely,
Stephen Collins

❧   Stephen Collins stars as Eric Camden on the hit television show, *7th Heaven*. He is also the author of the suspense thrillers, *Eye Contact* and *Double Exposure*.

Dear J. D.:

I went through high school during the second blush of *Catcher* readers when "I'm OK, You're OK" Transactional Psychology infiltrated our teachers' workshops. They were convinced that each of us was a ticking Holden Caulfield waiting to explode. Their pitying nods, the sympathetic, "Oh, dear, I *do* understand *unlike* those *teachers in The Catcher in the Rye*," overdone pats on our shoulders (presumably to bolster our splintering egos) — all of these were wasted on a bunch of sixteen-year-olds whose greatest angst was over roller-skating in the halls, kissing behind lockers, and cutting class in order to spend the day at the lake.

My friends and I weren't "troubled youth," and reading *Catcher* didn't make any of us want to end our lives nor appreciate them more. Come to think of it, most of the girls in our group thought Holden was too stuck on himself and that the females in the novel were too fragile for our liking. But your fiction made our teachers squirm. Then, between the beat generation and Vietnam protest years (those would come later), we plotted over cafeteria lunches, finding ways to make our teachers worry that one of us would hop a bus to New York where she would spray-paint existentialist graffiti on subway walls before leaping onto the tracks in front of a fast-approaching train.

In college, between protest marches down at Gazebo Square, I read *Franny and Zooey.* Franny drove my feminist side crazy with her inane chanting of the Jesus Prayer. Enamored of Zooey, however, I called my mother by her first name, "Look, Patsy, you just don't get anything, do you?" Never mind that my mother had not read *Franny and Zooey* and, refusing to play Bessie to my Zooey, grounded me for a week "for being disrespectful." The voices of Zooey, Buddy, and Holden fueled my English major penchant for the geeky and the cheeky. I found kindred spirits who tossed off literary allusions with aplomb, who quoted Jay Gatsby as if he were their best friend, and who were above the rest of their peers. Your characters fed my narcissism right through the years I was becoming a writer.

After *Catcher* hit the markets, wherever you went, someone photographed you and published your image over captions like, "Famed Writer Salinger Takes Leak on Boardwalk." As much as such fame is alluring, your seclusion acknowledges what all of us as public writers face daily: every day a writer takes off all her clothes and stands in Times Square and waits — either they'll throw rocks at her or tell her how voluptuous she is; or worse, they won't notice her clothes are off. But to not step into the Square, to not even go downtown? There's the stuff my writerly dreams are made of, particularly when rejections have been too frequent or I've got three editors-in-waiting.

Those nights when I crawl up the steps well past 2:00 A.M. collapsing into bed, my back aching with lines I just could not get right yet, I fall asleep dreaming Salinger dreams. In them, I have sold "The Big One" and thus gone into quiet hermitage to write beyond the restraints of critics and merciless readers. I grow wizened and wise and finally die. Upon opening my writing desk drawers, loved ones are greeted by volumes and volumes of the World's Best Writing.

Thanks for the reality and imagination,
K. T. Fischer

❦ Katherine Fischer lives along the banks of the Mississippi River in Dubuque, Iowa. She teaches creative writing at Clarke College.

Dear JD:

I'm sitting in a phone booth at Port Authority in midtown Manhattan. I've been walking down Broadway since I woke up some time after midnight, from the cheap hotel where I'm staying on 92nd Street near Riverside, and morning rush hour is going full bore now outside. I couldn't care less. I'm listening to the guy in the booth next to me. Mid-50s or so, clean-shaven, casual but cleanly dressed, he's talking to me about Kant, Picasso, Joyce, history, and the importance of art. I can't believe it's happening. I'm eight-een, just done with my freshman year at college, a midwesterner in New York City for the first time ever. I was supposed to meet a friend at the hotel, but our signals got crossed and I'm alone. But I'm not worried; being in these streets, in the likes of conversations like this, is better than I'd even imagined. From the guy who propositioned me in the hotel lobby, to the guy hustling three-card monte, to the glass of beer I can have as an eighteen-year-old here, to the cops banging up the dozers I was sitting with on the waiting room benches, this is what amazing means for me. This is what I came for. This is what I meant when I wrote on my college applica-tion essay that the most important influence on my life was your book. Okay, so it wasn't true; but that just made the idea even more fitting. The main thing that Holden Caulfield knows is that it's all phony, right?

William Burroughs said that *On the Road* had sold a million Levi's, put a generation on the highway, and he may have been right. But even before Sal Paradise went looking for enlightenment, Holden Caulfield quit school and wandered the city streets, just as hungry. Everyone who reads knows about the Beat Generation, and the postwar complacency that Kerouac, Ginsberg, Burroughs & Co. protested. But Holden Caulfield's disaffection is perhaps even sharper; he doesn't have a Dean Moriarty or anyone to show him a way. Or maybe it's just that he didn't have a Ginsberg to press his case. Either way it's a cry nearly as old as language, heard in our time with particular urgency.

When we say we wish you had gone on, had written more, had published more for us, what we're really saying is that the search never ends. But you gave us what you had to, and we're lucky, those of us who could, to have read it. And so, today I'm in Paris, staying in one of the small, old hotels a short Metro ride from the city center. My own fourteen-year-old son is in the next room, reading your book, and thinks it's great. A Catalan café is across the street, a chocolatier, a flower store on each side of it. Horns and voices and traffic keep pouring through the window. Last night after late supper at another café down the street, he and the friend of his who came with us got on their skateboards, took off for an hour or more and came back, downright exhilarated. Of course nothing lasts; but some things do go on, at least for a while.

All I can say is thank you.
Barry Silesky

❦   Barry Silesky's books include *One Thing That Can Save Us* (short-short fiction) and *Ferlinghetti: The Artist in His Time* (a biography). He runs *Another Chicago Magazine* and teaches writing and literature at the School of the Art Institute of Chicago.

Dear Mr. Salinger-

I have read *The Catcher in the Rye* a half dozen times, and each time I'm
older, though it's still reading fine — right now, it's raising pimples on my
thirty-somethin' face, I feel the queasy sting of adolescence on this dirty
subway's space, you get me all pent up — and I'm enjoying the self
loathing, I've spun my hat right round backwards and made fun of
stranger's clothing — I survived the ride, stumbling tonight, now walking
through the streets, like a juvenile outsider and I left your book on the
subway seat — I'm feeling Holden Caulfield — he's in my fucking skin,
he does this every time, with that stupid shit-faced grin — I'm just a punk
student running from a class, skipping out of school, getting called a stupid ass by parents, friends, cabbies — the whole damn world's straighter
than me, I'm drunk, all crooked lines, and I'm fucked by my own whimsy.

What pisses me off the most is you wrote this brilliant book, so good some
asshole decided to give John Lennon too hard a look and that's the thing
with god damn art — it either brings you to yourself, or it pulls you right
apart.

God damn, the book is great and here is my apology — it should have
never been a tool for reworking God's astrology — some people are chosen
for great, great deeds, some hearts were meant to bleed and bleed, and
old Holden Caulfield thought he was both, and so did the guy who's gun
stepped close, and what a fucking shame, cause I bless this book, your
heart, your name — there's part of me in every page, that dignified my
teenage rage — but the bullets, man, they weren't that smart — the finger
pulled back on art — the bullets went where they were pointed, like they
tend to do, left the killer on the sidewalk, with your book, he's reading
you . . .

He's where he belongs,

And I'm still singing Lennon's songs

And if you want to take a look,

On my shelf resides another copy

Of your potent, ageless book

Thank you for your work, it helped me through a harder time, when I couldn't speak a single word of why I felt so blind — to myself — this little book was like a big-ass mirror that gave this boy some faith, by God, and made the world a little clearer.

I'm a musician, and I write what I see, and who I am, and what I want the world to be, and that, Mr. Salinger, is all she be — that's what your little book taught me.

> *Highest regards,*
> *Ellis Paul*

Ellis Paul is a songwriter and musician. He grew up in northern Maine. His latest album is called *Live*.

Dear J. D. Salinger,

I picture you as a wild

recorder of music taping

the latest punk rock from

the radio, Holden-style,

never giving up the ghost

of your creativity, writing

now song lyrics with a Zen

base, something like "incantations

for a punk meditation" staying

up all night with those sounds

charging your lonely haunt

and dancing like Seymour

while your voice in a tape

recorder translates the

rhythms and images into

Zen rock wild gyrations

dancing for yourself singing

for yourself though something

for posterity like one day

on that all-night punk station

there will be the Salinger hour

and the zombie crew will know

the meaning of "the sound of

one finger snapping"

> *Your spirit brother,*
> *Tony Moffeit*

Tony Moffeit is poet-in-residence at the University of Southern Colorado in Pueblo. He is also a blues singer.

Dear J. D. Salinger,

Following are two poems from my continuing series called "Chinese Notes" I offer you in small return for the pleasure and insight your work has given me.

Two Chinese Notes for J. D. Salinger

I'd be confined

to dreams

were it

not

for the

blue dragonfly

just landed

on

my hand

*

Creek

crawling through

woods

How many thousands

of years

without stopping

I'm happy

to listen

longer

than that

*

Yours sincerely,
Barry Gifford

❧   Barry Gifford is a novelist and screenwriter. His works include *Wild at Heart*, *Lost Highway*, and *American Falls*.

Dear Mr. Salinger,

Yesterday, my boyfriend and I were having lunch, and I started to feel
these pressure points in my head, and sharp tingling all over my upper
arms and abdomen. I wanted a drink, but Rich didn't have money to cover
the extra stuff. So I swallowed a Xanax in private and told myself that it was
just a phase. I bet you know what it's like firsthand to talk to a man
absorbed by his own intellect and the last slippery little shit on a plate full
of sea shells. Well, that's what it's like talking to Rich. Sometimes I just let
him have the whole conversation. He talks a lot about morality plays and
the modern American novel. He works part-time at a law firm in Omaha,
and sometimes he talks about the books he reads at night. I think it's so
goddam ironic that he likes your books and I bet he's never even read
Franny and Zooey. If he had, he wouldn't talk like such a hot-shot. I suppose I shouldn't talk. I'm a regular goddam Holden Caulfield with the
religious obsession of Franny Glass. But I'm not picky like Rich. I know if
there had been anything exotic on the menu at lunch yesterday, like frog
legs or escargot or flaming cheese or sushi he would have ordered it.
Instead, he got the most expensive whiskey, which happened to be Wild
Turkey, and a hot roast beef sandwich. At least it wasn't a strawberry crepe
or some Parisian crap like that. Rich just got back from a semester in
Lyon, and he's always giving me advice on French fashion, how long to
wear my skirts and how to say important things like, *Dans la vie, c'est
nécessaire d'avoir des amis, mais il ne faut pas avoir de l'argent*. I wish I
could just tell him what an ass he makes of himself when he talks like a
hairy old professor.

To tell you the truth, I almost exploded yesterday. Right there in that goddam café in front of everyone. I almost did it right in front of that law clerk
friend of his, when she came over to brag about her shitty little internship
in the judge's office. I didn't have time for her shit. It was four months
since Rich and I had seen each other, and all we'd been talking about was
Rich, Rich, Rich. Besides that, it was shitty little comments like what a
honky tonk café we were in. He kept pointing out some smudge of eye-

liner that ran across my cheekbone every time I itched my left eye. He told me to quit talking about art school. He said if I knew what the real world was like, I wouldn't be making these *life-changing* decisions without really thinking through them.

I wanted to do something desperate, so I said we should break up. Then I said all those cutesy little things like we didn't have anything in common anymore and we were growing apart and we needed time to think things over. I think I even said some goddam shit about the fact that he liked morality plays and I liked romance novels (which I don't). Besides that, I told him I couldn't stand sushi and even though cubism was politically correct, I still liked Frangelico. He just blinked a lot when I said that crap, like he was pretending to understand but was more interested in his roast beef sandwich. Then he said something like, "You need to stop thinking about this whole art mess. Your parents don't want it, and neither do I. I'm going to law school in the fall, and we need money if we get married."

I wanted a cold glass of water, but the waitress hadn't been by in over forty-five minutes.

Then I decided I didn't have to make up phony shit to make him believe we shouldn't be together. There were *real* issues.

I told him my sister's second baby had died. He didn't say much, just "I'm sorry." Then he said something about the Dodgers winning the pennant but that their pitcher was traded which didn't bode well for next season.

Then I told him I'd stopped taking my medication. He just looked at me and said I looked thinner and that maybe that was a good thing. I couldn't even remember if I'd ever told him I *was* taking medication. My belly got tight, and my arms got worse. It must have been that goddam coffee, but still, it might be that it's two weeks since I stopped taking the meds.

I went to the bathroom to see if I had any more Xanax. I sat on the toilet like Franny and watched the door swing open and closed when some lady would come in to use the bathroom or apply makeup or wash her hands. I started thinking that I only wanted to become an artist because I thought I *had* to, and it didn't even feel good to stroke the brush or smudge the charcoals on the canvas anymore. It didn't even feel right. It was like mouthing the words to the national anthem.

And I'm under a lot of stress — you know, the usual. I have an application to finish, and I'm not exactly enjoying nursing school. To tell you the truth, I'm seriously considering dropping it all and going to art school. But Rich says I'll make a much better nurse. He complimented me once about the drawings in the back seat of my Buick Park Avenue, but he said I should do my artwork on the side. I'd never make a good living carrying around an easel on some lonely-ass seaside boardwalk. Besides that, I've missed the deadline for financial aid and even if I get in on late admissions, I'll have to work full-time to pay for school. I don't know why exactly I want to do this, but it's like I want to feel consumed by something difficult. There's this goddam nagging inside me that God wants me to stop nursing school and become an artist, to show the world what I can do and be famous and independent, like Andy Warhol or Georgia O'Keefe or some other hot-shot like that. That's what I was thinking about on the toilet. It was a no-smoking bathroom, but I lit up. I smoke a lot, but I justify it by a priest I knew who used to smoke a pack a day. I guess that makes me more of a Holden, but shit, I still have Franny's scruples. I used to be able to scare myself by making faces in the mirror. I used to believe everything any adult told me. One time, my housemother at boarding school told me that *modernism* was sweeping over the country, like a *black plague.* Every state school professor she knew had been a goddam liberal, and even the ones at private schools were phonies. It would take a very strong Catholic to survive the persecution these liberals inflicted, and Sister Mary Augustine said I'd fold. I'd read in one of her books that I was no more than a maggot in the sight of God. My soul was black from original, mortal, and venial sin. I think I *believed* I was a helpless maggot in the sight of God and that's why by senior year, I really *was* having trouble doing things on my own. Waking up was a goddam chore, I nearly failed sociology, and I lost fifteen pounds in three months. It was Jansenism at best, goddam Jansenism and if I'd seen that, I might have rebelled. I might have left and gone to *public* school. But I wanted to hide in my dorm room where the Jesuits used to sleep. I swear I used to hear them breathing at night in the winter, but then it occurred to me that it was only the paint chips peeling away from my goddam flimsy walls. I thought I'd be safe if I could just lie there in bed, and avoid all those evil things outside — false apparitions, the punishment of natural disasters, and let's not forget devil worship. I wanted a goddam ivory tower, where nothing could touch my *pious aphorisms and penitent ejaculations.*

I know I'm lousy right now, but it's just that *I'm sick of ego, ego, ego.* Religious ego, intellectual ego, moral ego . . . *everyone's ego including my own.*

So, I guess I'm asking your advice. Would you say Rich is a phony? And is it a goddam crapshoot to run off to art school? I know I'm hardly in a position to say so myself, but I'm not institution material. I've survived two weeks without the meds. Sometimes I get those tingles, but every now and then, things look crystal clear. The other night I just lay in my bed thinking, sorting through that goddam high school mess, and all the other goddam shit about financial aid. I put a hot washcloth over my eyes, and that cleared my head a little. For a while, I was thinking about nothing.

I hope you can help.

> Sincerely,
> Ellen Fangman

❧ Ellen Fangman teaches literature at the University of Kansas in Lawrence. She has published poetry, art, and criticism in small journals and looks forward to finishing graduate school.

Dear Mr. Salinger:

I was shaking slightly by the time I got to the bookstore. Too much coffee on an empty stomach. I went immediately to the classics section, and of course they didn't have *The Catcher in the Rye*. Another lady in a trench coat was also looking for it. I went ahead and ordered it anyway. But I wanted a copy of that book now, so I called this other bookstore, right? The lady on the phone said they had an old paperback copy. "Look, there's this other lady looking for it," I told her, "Can you hold it for me?" "Sure," she said. "What's your name?" "Caulfield." I spelled it for her.

Here I am driving a beat-up truck with expired out-of-state tags, only one working headlight and a clutch that's about to go out. I haven't even filed my taxes from last year and I'm on a mad dash to the bookstore, so you can imagine where my priorities are.

I've probably owned at least five copies of that book. I can remember at least two different copies — one red and white — and even one copy I found with all of the cuss words blacked out with a magic marker. You should've seen it. It looked like some badly declassified government document. The copy I bought today, when I finally got to it, was old as hell — 1961, nineteenth printing, 50¢ cover price, yellowing pages, and a cheesy painted cover with a guy wearing his hat backwards and a lady in the background smoking a cigarette. In bold letters it said "This unusual book may shock you, will make you laugh, and may break your heart — but you will never forget it." No shit, Sherlock. If they published a book with every letter from someone who laughed out loud while reading it and cried at the end it would make that guy who wrote *The Rise and Fall of the Roman Empire* blush.

"The only thing is, it's $2.50," the woman behind the counter informed me, like that was some astronomical price for such an old copy of one of the greatest books ever written. "I don't care *how* much it is," I told her, semidefying her to escalate it. She laughed kind of, and said "Of course you do," which struck me as right at the very heart of what the book was about in the first place. But then again, I tend to analyze things too much.

Sometimes my wheels spin so much you can almost hear them. I have a friend who's an editor at a magazine and she says I have too many antennas. She says it in a conspiratorial manner, like "It's okay to have too many antennas, David, but just watch out for yourself a little bit better in the future."

I know several *several* Holden Caulfields. One of 'em is in jail for driving under the influence and having a bad attitude. One of 'em teaches math but really only cares about music. He's spent the last ten years of his life holed up in his apartment drinking beer and listening to obscure British bands. Another one is this girl I met in Florida who only wears combat boots and is so pretty I had to squint whenever I looked at her. I did pretty much anything she wanted me to during the year we went out together, but of course that wasn't enough so we're not together anymore. Like me, she's got some issues she needs to work out. And *me*? If I was Arthur Miller, the name of my play would be *Death of a Temp*. I'm not an administrative assistant or managing editor of anything. I have a degree in English literature and yet I never had any plans to teach. I just knew how to write papers and read books written prior to the twentieth century without finding them boring. I'm not "online" and I work in an office with nothing but computer terminals where being hooked into the "information revolution" means you still make six dollars an hour with no benefits. Without being a member of the literati or the liberally-educated intelligentsia or the last bastion of cultural free expression or whatever they call themselves and having no great call in life I know *The Catcher in the Rye* was written for me.

I have this uncanny ability to say something too disturbing or revealing about myself or the general scheme of things usually within the first five minutes of conversations and usually without ever fully realizing it. I never mean any harm by it, but I'm always misunderstood if there's a chance to be misunderstood. I always find my mark. So, as far as I'm concerned, Holden Caulfield is the one that makes sense and the world around him and *you* and *me* are the ones that are screwed up. I never grew up past the mental landscape I see in your stories. I wear hats that people think are

Dear Mr. Salinger,

A letter typically has some kind of purpose, and I don't know what I seek from you by writing this. When I was a kid I always planned to write you and tell you how great you were, imagining that you would be so moved by my understanding of you and your writing that you'd invite me to come hang out with you. I would become your literary protégé, and . . . ah, anyway, I read somewhere that you regularly got bushels of such letters and just dumped them all unopened into a garbage can at the P.O. I didn't think that was true, but it planted enough doubt in my head to prevent me from ever actually writing to you. I was a lazy kid in some ways.

I read a lot as a kid though. My dad had moved our family from Chicago to a house in the middle of the woods in rural Illinois so he could get in touch with nature and write haiku. There weren't any kids around to play with, so I read books. By the time I'd reached fifth grade I'd read every volume of Hardy Boys in the school library, and had burned through all the Twain and Jack London. Then my tastes took an unfortunate twist. I began accompanying my mom on her trips to Kmart, where I would buy paperback novels, the covers of which usually featured a James Bond–type (though he usually looked younger and considerably more mercenary than 007) holding a sleek and blazing machine gun in the crook of one arm, and an alarmed girl wearing a torn bikini in the other. My dad was too savvy to censor my tastes, so he instead tried to influence them. He drove me to the county library and sent me inside to check out your novel, the one about the teenage boy who gets kicked out of school.

The librarian told me to take a hike. She possessed none of the let-kids-read-what-they-want spirit I had found at Kmart. I couldn't check out your book, so I had to call my dad inside to do it. He couldn't believe it. Neither could I. I was furious. But as eager as I was to defy that librarian, I had my doubts about your novel, I must admit. I did not consider my dad a square at all. It just seemed unlikely that we would have the same tastes in literature. The drive home from the library did nothing to dispel those fears. At every stoplight he'd grab the book from me and start flipping though it.

"Hahahaha . . . 'Cold as a witch's teat.' I love that line. God, this is a great book."

I started to get a little uneasy. It became clear that he wasn't simply trying to clean up my reading list — he was looking for a buddy to share his absolute love of your book with. Well, I figured, I can just pretend I like it.

That, of course, wasn't necessary. I'm hoping to somehow heighten the sincerity of this fan letter by leaving out any of the usual testimonies. I'll just say this: I realized, only a page or so into it that I had a gloriously fun future ahead of me — I was going to be a fiction writer!

I never did any fiction writing, though, until age sixteen when my elderly high school English teacher Mrs. Gorsky assigned our class to write a couple short stories. I tackled the assignment with a vigor I'd never experienced before. One of the stories I wrote dealt with a ninth grader who goes to see a basketball game between his school and a rival team. The rival school is where his junior high school sweetheart, Chrissy, went after graduation split them apart. He stays up all night thinking about how it will be to finally see her again. When he does see her though, she has changed. She's a cheerleader. Her greeting is icy and brief. I think, as I read that story after finishing it, I actually wept with sympathy for this fictional boy, so palpably real did I find his suffering.

The other story, I must confess, was about a little boy with a pet goldfish. He lived in a city high-rise apartment with wealthy, somewhat emotionally distant parents. One day his father brings home a little goldfish in a bag and rather awkwardly presents it to the boy. The boy names it Freddy. The boy is regularly stricken with nightmares from which he awakens in such a dismal cloud of existential despair that he cries openly and goes to his parents for comfort. They want to know why he is crying. Thinking they will only understand a concrete explanation, he always blames it on the fish, saying "Freddy bit me."

The boy's only true human connection is with the "colored" maid. She is a warm, sensual person, and never fails to cheer the boy up with her good humor. One day, though, she surprisingly breaks down in tears while telling the boy that it isn't the nightmares that hurt, it's the waking up from happy dreams. For some reason that's the last he sees of her. About that same time he has another nightmare, but his father tells him straight out that if he hears any more reports of that fish biting anyone, he's going to have him put to sleep.

This is such an embarrassingly obvious riff on "The Secret Goldfish" that I'm hesitant to even bring it up. But it seems pretty germane. Anyway, Mrs. Gorsky pulled me aside and told me I should consider becoming a writer. "Consider?" I thought to myself, "Babe . . . you have no idea who you're talking to." Who, in fact, was she talking to? Why, the next J. D. Salinger, of course.

But things changed in my life pretty dramatically shortly after my chat with Mrs. Gorsky, and my glorious career as a writer was put on hold. My parents got divorced, I ran away from home, got kicked out of school, spent some time living in my car, and finally, when I turned eighteen, signed up for the army. My car broke down on the side of the road one night, and I hitched a ride to a friend's house, planning to go get the car the next day. By the time I got back to it, though, it had been towed, and I didn't have the money to bail it out. I had to leave for boot camp. There wasn't anything very valuable in that car. Aside from a cardboard box in the trunk containing the story about the goldfish.

That was a long time ago, but I doubt a month has gone by that I haven't thought about that damn goldfish story. I wouldn't even think of trying to rewrite it. My life took a lot of unexpected turns since I handed it in to Mrs. Gorsky. And when I finally got down to being a writer, years later, I was a different person. I wrote a novel, and when it eventually got published, a lot of critics did note the influence of your book. One review though, probably the best one, concentrated on the differences between the boy in my book (Alex Verdi) and the boy in yours. I received a surprise letter from Mrs. Gorsky just last week and she asked me an odd question: "Who do you think you are more like — Alex Verdi or Holden Caulfield?" Well, about all I can say is when I look back at things, there are some people I just don't miss at all. No, sir. Not yet, anyway. I'll tell you what I do miss though — that story about the goldfish. Goddammit, that may have been the best thing I ever wrote. That's what my dad tells me anyway, and, you know, I've come to trust his opinion on these things.

Very Best,
Don De Grazia

❦ Don De Grazia's debut novel is called *American Skin*. He teaches creative writing at Columbia College in Chicago.

Dear Mr. Salinger,

In 1970, a bookmobile traveled up my dirt road twice a month. By age eleven I'd read every book on its shelves. I was then allowed to accompany my mother to town once a week, where she shopped for groceries and I visited the newly-opened library. There was a four-book limit per library card, but I got around that by getting cards in my siblings' names, two of whom could not read. I read sixteen books a week. My all-time favorite was *Harriet the Spy* because it was about a little girl who carried pencil and paper and wrote notes about her friends. I loved the genre of misfit kids who came out ahead. The best books involved a boy who hit the winning homerun and suddenly everyone liked him. All I really wanted was acceptance and I found it through reading.

The town library was staffed by volunteers and one afternoon an ancient woman would not leave me alone. She insisted on helping me find books, an endeavor I preferred to do alone. Out of politeness, I allowed her to dig around in the card catalog for me under the heading, "Baseball." There were too many books and she asked me to narrow my interest. I told her my favorite player was Johnny Bench, catcher for the closest big league team, the Cincinnati Reds. She continued to flip cards and I continued to wait with growing impatience. Finally she led me to a part of the library I had not yet explored and removed a book from the shelf. I dutifully checked it out along with my other fifteen books. After supper I opened the book. It was *The Catcher in the Rye*.

I stayed up all night reading that book. It literally changed my life. I didn't know a book could be that way — honest, about real life, and with the word "goddam" on the first page. This was not a book about a made-up misfit kid who suddenly everyone liked; here was a genuine misfit who did the best he could — same as me. I never read another juvenile book again.

Chris Offutt

❧ Chris Offutt is the author of two collections of stories, *Kentucky Straight* and *Out of the Woods*, a novel, *The Good Brother*, and a memoir, *The Same River Twice*.

Dear Holden,

I read your book *The Catcher in the Rye* when I was fourteen, the year
before my first child was born, which is like forty-two years ago (if you
want to know the truth). My favorite English teacher, Mr. Griffin, at
Everett Junior High (in San Francisco's Mission District), who was obviously gay and the sweetest guy, gave us the name of your book to read. He
was so nice and really cared about all of us (mostly Mexican and black,
poor white, with only an occasional and rare white middle-class kid) so
that no one made not one (usual) nasty or mean fourteen year old snicker.
I mean, no one ever made fun of him even in private as far as I knew. And
he used to say about my very weird short stories, "You could be a writer,
Alma, it takes a lot of work, but you could." And I thought, this guy is nuts.
Nice, but whacko. Me a writer, for sure . . .

And so, I'd read lots of boring "good books" (literature), and pretty interesting "good books" (again literature . . . I was in the highest track where the
kids could actually read) — but when I opened your book, Holden, I
thought Mr. Griffin had really screwed up this time. It was so interesting,
so funny, and like someone was just sitting around telling me their own
real life, the unvarnished truth, no lies, no BS, not literature, but a great
story. And you were about my age (though of course you're a boy) — it felt
like everything you said was just popping out of my own brain. I had to put
your book down a bunch of times so I could just crack up (you were that
hilarious . . . remember Old Sonny, Old Phoebe, your old teachers . . .).
It was like you were wearing X-ray glasses and no one had succeeded in
teaching you to lie socially, but most importantly you weren't lying to
yourself.

Then, toward the end of the book I guess I started to realize how lonely
you probably were, like how when you talked about your little sister, "Old
Phoebe," I could tell how much you really loved and missed her. You just
said the truth — it's no picnic growing up (especially if your parents are

always trying to give you away, I understood that). And at the end when you were remembering everyone and of course missing them (even if they were a bunch of phonies). I remember wishing we could go to Golden Gate Park, have tea in the Japanese Tea Garden, rent a bike (I could've taken you to the secret places I found as a kid), go to have three or four hot dogs — with tons of relish and mustard squishing out — with sweet, icy sodas; and then we could've rode the merry-go-round. We could've hopped the horses in a complete circle and been fast and sneaky enough to switch horses when the merry-go-round sheriff wasn't looking. If he caught you, you were banned for the day. You could've called him Old Charlie or Old Harry . . . but I had no way to reach you. I didn't know about writing in care of the publisher in those days — I didn't even know where to buy a stamp.

And then when you said that thing in *The Catcher in the Rye*, about how you would stand at the edge of the cliff saving kids — for some reason I really can't ever explain, it comforted me to think that somewhere some-one like a catcher in the rye was there just in case. And I think what hap-pened is that after I had three kids by the age of twenty-one, I kind of became a catcher in the rye . . . did that happen to you too, Holden? Did you become a parent and stand at the edge of a cliff for the rest of your life, saving kids? I know, you're thinking, what a stupid question, like how would I eat, sleep, watch TV, read, write more stories, have a family and just live a regular life if I were always standing on some stupid cliff. Sorry, I had to ask. But I want you to know I gave your book to my kids when they got to be about thirteen. I could hear them cracking up as they read and reread; your book really got worn-out-looking.

I just wanted you to know if I could've gotten hold of you somehow I really would've taken you to my secret places in Golden Gate Park. And a funny thing is, now that all my kids are twenty years and older, you're the only one who stays about sixteen forever to me. If you can find a stamp write back — I don't know if I could've kept telling myself the unvarnished, no lie, no BS truth without your book, Holden, and guess what . . . I turned out to be a writer like Old Mr. Griffin said (and he was right, lots of work).

One more thing — did you ever find out if the ducks freeze overnight in that pond in winter? For years I kept imagining them stuck and frozen like duck popsicles all night until the sun came, if the sun came out. Maybe the only way to find out is to camp by a pond where ducks hang out in the winter (see what you started . . .).

But Holden, thanks for being your true sixteen-year-old self forever — it helps me remember who I really (no BS) am. Not a catcher in the rye, but a human trying to see the truth no matter what happens or how bad it gets. And now that I'm writing you, forty-two years later, I really miss you . . .

Old Alma
XXOO

❦   Alma Luz Villanueva is the author of seven books of poetry, including *Desire* and *Vida*. She teaches creative writing at Antioch University in Los Angeles, California.

Dear Mr. Salinger,

Do you ever wonder how a novel about a rich prep school kid in Manhattan — troubled by a traumatic family event and now talking to a psychiatrist — became *the* classic novel about American youth angst and coming-of-age? Do you wonder how people related to a world which, frankly, is not the world where most of us have ever lived? I have a brilliant graduate student who grew up in the ghettos of New Jersey in the 1980s — never knew her father, often homeless, taking care of her stoned mother even when she was a toddler. I wonder if she read *Catcher*, did she find something there that spoke directly to her? Conversely, do you wonder if upper-middleclass teenagers today would care about saving innocent children from the realities of life; would they want to make being a "catcher" their role in life? A popular radio talk-show host says that adolescent males are "the most dangerous animal on earth." Part of me agrees . . . part of me wonders if there is still a world where a gentle Holden Caulfield can be honestly distressed about peers who might be too fast with a girl he met last summer on Long Island or the Cape. And how did this world ever touch *me*?

In the 1970s when I was in high school, everything (in class) had to be *relevant*. That was the buzzword, the quality by which our interest was earned. A slice of the baby-boomer generation who didn't face draft into the Vietnam war, we were bored with our lives and restless for something to care about (to rebel against). The senior prom was almost cancelled due to lack of interest. There was no dress code and boys and girls dressed identically in Levi's and corduroys and proletarian work shirts. We hadn't the slightest idea what a hound's tooth coat was, nor would the boys have worn one on a date. Our public high school in a semirural county in Southern California couldn't be farther from Holden's prep school and upper west side of Manhattan. And yet *Catcher* passed the "relevant" test. It did so because a decade before, parents (not *our* parents, but that would've been better) were up-in-arms, even had meetings, to try to prevent the school from using *Catcher* as a classroom text. We had no idea what they found objectionable in the book, nevertheless felt smug and superior, and while it wasn't the book we carried in our rear pockets to manifest our "voice" (that, I believe, was *Zen and the Art of Motorcycle Maintenance*), it was the book that incited some of us, like Holden, to tell our stories in our own honest, naïve, earnest, digressive voices. Actually ours were imitations of Holden's voice, but despite the difference in worlds, his voice, it seemed, *sounded* like ours. So we took it. I took it.

But what about girls' experiences — how had this book become significant to *us*? (And why weren't we reading *Franny and Zooey* as well?) In high school English, there were exactly two books with female main characters: Abigail and other girls accused of being witches in *The Crucible*, and Hester Prynne, an adulteress, in *The Scarlet Letter*. Talk about lack of relevance. We dragged our asses through those books. It was Huck Finn and Nick Romano and Nick Adams and Holden Caulfield who we "related to." So when my teacher read my first short story, narrated in a familiar frank first person adolescent voice, and asked me why the narrating character was a boy, I answered "Because I think it's more significant that this happened to a boy and he feels this way."

No, I don't blame you for teaching me that lesson. Yes, I got over the weird conception, although I've read that girls still show similar symptoms. I also recovered from my tenaciously held conviction that I couldn't write in anything other than the ardent first person voice of an adolescent. Maybe the most lasting thing *Catcher* gave me was the developing notion: I can write; this is what I want to do; this is what I *will* do. Obviously *Catcher* was a book, and Holden a character, that transcended historical era, social-economic class, *and gender*.

But do you ever wonder if it transcended race as well?

Warm regards,
Cris Mazza

🦋   Cris Mazza is the author of nine books of fiction. Her most recent novel, *Girl Beside Him*, was released in 2001.

Dear Mr. Salinger:

Here I am, past fifty, and I just met you on paper, and I'm thinking wow, where has this guy been all my life? How come that during all of my fancy schooling and my double master's degrees and all of my talk and work in English literature I never met you? I don't know. It seems as though you were always there, on the outskirts, somewhere in my understanding of Americana. Even as I was growing up in Asia, I heard about you. But I never got around to doing anything about it. In America, my teenaged daughter kept insisting I read *The Catcher in the Rye*, yet I never did. Then, this year, with Holden Caulfield's adventure book turning fifty, my desk at my newspaper office in Milwaukee became a veritable shrine to him — and to you. Stories about you or that Caulfield boy started coming over the wires, and I began to wonder: What's all this fuss about? And why are all these people making all this noise over a writer who never wants to see or talk to anyone or even publish anything anymore?

So then I went to the bookstore, and bought *The Catcher in the Rye* in paperback. And now I'm half in love with Holden Caulfield myself and, just as he ached to phone the writers he admired, I want to rush over and talk to his creator. I guess that means you.

I want to tell you that twenty-one years ago, when I was sworn in as a U.S. citizen, the Daughters of the American Revolution welcomed me to my new country with miniature versions of the Stars and Stripes and coffee and cakes and little booklets about my rights and responsibilities and such. They should have saved their flags and their coffee, and given me just one book — *The Catcher in the Rye*. Every young newcomer to this country should read that one. It's more American than American pie, better than the American Heritage Dictionary, more relevant than Dr. Spock and Dr. Ruth put together, and it definitely, *definitely* tops any old guidebook to the Big Apple. Holden also would have prepared me for the three American teenagers I was to raise. And I suspect he would have helped me understand my deer-hunting, steer-loving, rule-breaking American husband much better.

I wonder if my life would have been any different had I read your definitive story of teenage turmoil in America at a time I myself was experiencing teenage angst in India. But I hadn't heard much about you then. It seems that I've been missing you everywhere — in bookstores, in libraries, at my high school, even in college. In my hometown of Mandalay, in what is now called Myanmar, I spent my pocket money in a dusty bookstore run by a betel nut–chewing Indian. I was about twelve or thirteen then. And I bought encyclopedias and books like *Treasure Island* and World War II novels there. I never came across your name. And no one told me about you.

Do you suspect there's a reason why no one told me? In the late '50s and early '60s wouldn't *Catcher* have been considered risqué? Especially in an Asian culture? I was then attending a Catholic boarding school in the Indian Himalayas and I don't know if the nuns would have let us read about Holden Caulfield. His swearing alone would have horrified them! Besides, Mr. Salinger, you are American. Our orientation was to the British. And so, I read George Eliot and Shakespeare and Hardy and Dickens and Agatha Christie. I never found you in our school library — and believe me, I would have found you had you been there. I spent a lot of time in that library.

At Punjab University in India, where I studied English literature, they had us read some Americans — Hemingway and Fitzgerald, Twain, Tennessee Williams, Pound and Eliot and so on — but not you. I wonder why not you. My friends and I were reading Nabokov and even Harold Robbins (covered in brown paper, of course), but no one passed around your book.

My first memorable introduction to an American author came when I was nearly fourteen. Mrs. Kurlander, the wife of a U.S. foreign service officer in Mandalay and a family friend, gave me a copy of *Little Women*. Ah, a pivotal book. From then on, I always wanted to marry a professor, as Jo did in *Little Women*, and stand beneath an umbrella in the rain with him. And so, when the marriage proposals came from good Indian families for me, I held out. I had plans. No arranged marriage for me. I wanted my professor underneath the umbrella in the rain. But what if Mrs. Kurlander had given me *Catcher*?

Why didn't Mrs. Kurlander give me *Catcher*, which would have been so right for me? And what would my dream have been had she? Perhaps I would have accepted one of the proposals. There was one I remember from a Holden Caulfieldish tea planter who thought reading Aristotle was sort of phony. More likely, I would have looked for Holden Caulfield in the streets of New York. Now that I've finally met him in your book, I know I'd have said: To hell with the professor. I like this mixed up, crazy Holden boy. I like the way he thinks everyone else is phony, I like the way he wears his deer hunting cap, I like his voice, his sound.

The thing is Mr. Salinger, and I'm sure you already know this, Americans don't have the market on teenagedom. Holden Caulfield doesn't belong only to America. And he doesn't belong only to the 1950s. He's one of those Shangri-la types — forever fresh, from the fountain of youth. His alienation, his loneliness, his insecurities, his sadness, his flight from authority — this is not just an American language of teenagers.

Perhaps that's why, even at this age, your book held me. I remembered my own boarding school in the Himalayas, a Pencey twin in more than one way. We wore gym slips, saris and *salwar-kameezs* and ate curries and cutlets. But, secretly, in our hearts, we spoke a Caulfield language. We too said meaningless things to teachers, laying it on thickly. We too wanted to take flight and roam freely in big cities without telling our parents. And remember the part where Holden says that anytime a girl does something pretty he falls for her? Funny thing — we felt the same way about the boys in the boy's school over on the next Himalayan peak. Also, believe me, there were a lot of Ackleys and Stradlaters at my school. Isn't it strange how every school in every city in the world has these characters?

Finally, Mr. Salinger, I understand something I wouldn't have grasped had I read your book as a teenager. There's a Holden Caulfield buried somewhere in the adult American male. In fact, there's a little Holden Caulfield in all of us. That's the beauty, the paradox, of your book. It's a uniquely American story that's universal.

Please give us another one.

> *Sincerely,*
> *G. S. Jensen*

❦ Geeta Sharma-Jensen was educated in Burma, India, and in the United States. She has been a reporter for newspapers in Wisconsin since 1975.

Dear Mr. Salinger,

A stranger has asked me to write you this letter. Forgive me. I cannot do it. Every time I start, I think: *I need to write my own father.* I need to say: *My dearest . . .*

Today, snow fell in flakes huge and wondrous, clusters with wings that filled the sky, thousands of white butterflies. *Dear Daddy.* I met a woman whose laugh rippled out of her, a deep-throated burbling sound, a magic flute, the song of a Western Meadowlark, rising from tall grass. In Lubbock, the red Texas sun set and a boy with two mothers twirled me under his arm; for a moment, we danced. Later, I ate a bowl of perfect berries — blueberries and raspberries, strawberries, blackberries — there were enough for you and Mom and Gary and Wendy and Laurie, and I ate them all very slowly and I wished that you were there to eat them with me.

Daddy. I have a student named Hansel and another named Heidi. One Micah, one Fawn, the one and only La Flora Easter. In Ohio, I had a student who was also a grandfather and he was dying of brain cancer and he was writing every day and the stories of his life were letters to his children and grandchildren and his first grandson's name was Isaac Jerome and the name means *Merciful Laughter.*

My dear father. I am supposed to write a letter to J. D. Salinger, and I am writing to you instead, but I am thinking of a girl in one of his stories, a girl named Franny who longs to pray without ceasing, and what I want to tell you is that on days when snowflakes have wings, on days when I dance, when I love my students' names and my heart fills and I love all these people in my classroom and their names no longer matter, those days when a woman laughs like a bird, when the bowl of berries seems forever full, I am praying without words, without ceasing; I am struck dumb with awe and gratitude, and this is the only way I know to pray truly.

Just after Christmas, I walked in the park and saw a dog and a woman; the woman threw snowballs, and the dog chased them, mouth wide open, joyfully catching. One seagull by the shrinking pond held curls of fine red and green ribbon in its beak, and I asked it: *What are you wrapping?*

Sweet Father, you were there. I remember the summer you built the cabin and a robin made her nest on the strut where you meant to lay the final beam for the roof and you waited for the bright blue eggs to hatch, week after week, your project delayed but not denied, and the birds have been our blessing.

In "Zooey," there is a mother who brings her troubled daughter conse-crated chicken soup and a brother who tells her to drink it. Once upon a time, that same brother was a small boy who had to perform night after night, a contestant on a radio show called *It's a Wise Child,* a boy afflicted by his own precocious intelligence, a child suffering with knowledge who is saved at last by his beloved older brother. Seymour makes it all simple. He tells Zooey to shine his shoes for the Fat Lady in the studio audience, for that one woman who needs him most, for Jesus who is there, every-where and always, inside the woman, sitting in the dark among all who suffer, among all who are afflicted.

Dear Mr. Salinger. Thank you for these people who began to teach me when I found them nineteen years ago, who teach me still each time I pause to listen.

Last Sunday, a man in church held his sleeping child while he knelt and prayed and the man took the bread and the wine and the child woke and laughed and the laughter was merciful and Jesus was there, I promise, inside all of us.

Dear Daddy. Once upon a time, my nephew, your grandchild, told his mother, *I love you all the way up to God and all the way up to Grandpa.*

The primroses are scarlet with burning golden hearts. This is what I mean when I say my own heart bursts, when I say, *This is the heart of love, this is the heart of sorrow.*

> *My love to you*, my father, *all the way up to God, this day*
> *and forever and ever,*
> *your Melanie*

❧ Melanie Rae Thon's most recent book is the novel *Sweet Hearts*. Originally from Montana, she has taught at Emerson College, Syracuse University, and Ohio State University. She currently teaches at the University of Utah.

Dear Jerome,

I started thinking about you the same day I thought I believed in God. Christ on the cross sort of makes sense to me. What I mean is, if God came to earth, people would probably kill him, wouldn't they? Christ on the cross doesn't look likes he's figured much out, though, and I can't blame him because who has?

Speaking of people who died, my student's head was found in the mountains under a quaking aspen. He once told me he would rather stare at the sun all day than read one more word, so I gave my whole class an assignment to sit in a wheelchair in their pajamas, pretending to be old. Those who passed got to wear a colored metal star. I wonder what it would be like to be walking in the mountains and find somebody's little sun-warped head looking up at you. You would probably understand this kind of experience. I bet you would say, "Relax. Don't walk around if you aren't ready to see some heads." Then you would forget about it and go eat ten pieces of toast.

I guess you've heard that the sandpaper maker shot himself in the head while cleaning his civil war pistol. He thought he had himself a nice Colt revolver, but it was actually a Confederate gun and he would have known that if he had bothered to examine the serial numbers. It turned out that was the gun Jackie Gleason lost and missed so much.

About a hundred miles down the road, the zookeeper who wanted to be buried ended up, unfortunately, cremated instead. His liver sat in the pile of fluffy ashes completely untouched. Doesn't that sound like a miracle to you? My own liver would not be the size of a rabbit's if I could manage to stay away from the Pernod. I'd rather keep it wrapped up in a flag of Texas than carry it around inside me, but I know that there are those who just could not stand this. Those kinds of people like it when it rains all day. What do you think about rain?

Even though I'm always afraid that my plane will be struck by lightning, I flew to Drohobycz last week to sit on the grave of a writer buried under a wind chime shaped like a tripod. He was blown up when his spaniel retrieved a piece of dynamite instead of the gray goose he had anticipated. Word had it that he caught tuberculosis from a pointy-eared mountain squirrel, but this was later ruled an error and forgiven. His wife gave me one of his ties which, when I put it on, seemed a lovely sort of smoky red but now that I've been wearing it awhile, when knotted just right, it seems more like one of those colors you'd see if you had to live in a state where thunder sounded every time you took a book out of your back pocket.

If you're feeling bored, there is a book you will want to read. It's called *Tales from Reb Nachman: Parables Told by Rabbi Nachman of Breslov*. After reading it, I could not sleep for a long time. After the third night of insomnia, my legs were twitching and lights were popping in front of my eyes. When I finally fell asleep, I dreamed of a movie marquee that read, "If not now, when?" You should read that book. You really should.

Robert Burns

🦋 Robert Burns is an instructor of English at the United States Air Force Academy in Colorado Springs.

Dear Mr. Salinger:

Being private isn't the same as being humble. Or is it? Maybe in this noisy, nosy, hype-eager world those writers who remain silent in the face of their fame and critical acclaim automatically count as humble. It's hard to say. With art, with our own creations and the process of making them, or at least trying to make them, what else can we do except attempt to be humble and silent along the way? Of course what I'm saying here isn't really true. There have always been brilliant, wonderfully public writers. Think of Mark Twain. But you, Mr. Salinger, had to follow in the footsteps of the truly loud, the master of self-promo, of broken bones, of discarded wives and plane crashes, Hemingway, who eventually did himself in.

In any case, I'm sure none of the above has anything to do with your decision to lay low. Who knows what that's all about? We spin a web of conjecture around your silence — like electrons in their cloudy orbitals. We search for a formation. We imagine it, because that's all we can do. And in any case the ultimate silence — at least of your personal being and voice in bodily form, the final resolute silence — will soon come. Then your long, staid, hermitage up there in New Hampshire will seem loud in contrast. A noisy echo of the non-noise of your absence.

Let me say here that for a midwestern boy *The Catcher in the Rye* was not only an evocation of the charms and freedoms of the undercover cover of the bustling streets and cab rides, but it was also a direct invocation for all alienated Holdens wherever they might be: Come to New York, the book sang. Search out your little sister in Central Park. You'll find the truth here. At least you'll have a better shot in the city, the book sang. Sure, phonies swing around on the dance floors, but there is still — amid the grid of streets — a place where the redemptive nature of hiding can appear. Here you can reside incognito! Here you can sort your troubles! My first glimpse of who I might be, my first invitation to become urbane, to shed my midwestern garb (except for the hunting cap with the earflaps to remind me of the hinterlands), to become hopefully not a phony but someone versed in spotting the phonies, came from your book. Holden wasn't afraid to break away on his own, to find a certain silence, to sort and discard the false. He wasn't afraid to be frail, human, loving. His brother went off to Hollywood to sell out. But you, Mr. Salinger, stayed at home. You continued to move through the snowy city. Alone and silent. Devout and literary. You live. Thank God.

Sincerely,
David Means

🦋   David Means is the author of *A Quick Kiss of Redemption and Other Stories* and *Assorted Fire Events: Stories,* which was a finalist for the National Book Critics Circle Award in 2001. He teaches at Vassar College.

Memorandum for Record
To: JDS
Re: 1963, and now

"It was love at first sight."

"If I am out of my mind, it's all right with me, thought Moses Herzog."

"Lolita, light of my life, fire of my loins."

"Like all men, I tell a hundred lies a day."

On the lookout for unquelled first lines, I've kept a list. Heller, Bellow,
Nabokov, and Bourjaily, for instance, as above, have spots. In 1963, I began
collecting. I remember the year, not because President Kennedy was shot,
but because Gary Turner, a year ahead of me at Butte High, was on
Christmas break from Snow College, a Mormon college somewhere in
Utah. He arrived for break with a copy of *Catcher*.

> If you really want to hear about it, the first thing you'll probably want
> to know is where I was born, and what my lousy childhood was like,
> and how my parents were occupied and all before they had me, and all
> that David Copperfield kind of crap, but I don't feel like going into it,
> if you want to know the truth.

I was seventeen years old. The copy of *Catcher* I bought, I still have. It cost
$1.25. But: try to imagine my reading about eastern prep schools in Butte,
Montana. I mean, I went to high school with Evel Knievel — well, I knew
his brother who, as it turns out, was to fall to his death in a mineshaft, in
that mining city. And I: I was lucky enough after one summer to enroll in
college, like Gary. I'd worked at the 5,200 level of the Mountain Con
mine, one mile sunk into the earth — a long distance to fall. Gary never
worked a day in the mines. He was crippled.

"The Richest Hill on Earth," as Butte was dubbed, was, early on, the
largest city between St. Louis and Seattle. Mining barons became

Montana's first millionaires based on silver, then copper. By the 1880s, Butte was the world's biggest copper producer.

Some related facts: In 1899, Marcus Daly merged with Rockefeller's Standard Oil Company to create the Amalgamated Copper Mining Company. By 1910, having bought all remaining small mines, Amalgamated changed its name to the Anaconda Copper Mining Company. Butte's Miners Union formed in 1878, sending the largest delegation to the International Workers of the World's founding convention in Chicago in 1906. 1917: the city's population at a peak of 100,000, 168 men were killed in a mine fire — a fire that remains the worst mining disaster in American history. Three Heavyweight Champions: John L. Sullivan himself as well as Jim Jeffries and Bob Fitzsimmons all fought fights in Butte. All this to say there were no prep schools in my city. As you've already guessed, most of Butte's inhabitants were not barons or millionaires — they were schmuck miners. And boxers and gamblers and whores and bartenders and preachers and drunks.

We owned a cow in the city. Butte was a mining town, but *still*. Our house and field were not in the country. We lived two blocks from my grade school, a half-mile from our church. Lenz's Pharmacy and the Cobban Market (where my father and other miners had grocery tabs they could pay once a month) were practically neighbors. I dreamed of the sheriff coming to our house to tell my father it was illegal to keep cows. I didn't hold out much hope because at school we studied Montana history, and I knew there were more cows in my state than people and my teacher had informed us that Montana statutes dictated death by hanging for cattle rustling, but not for human murder. There were no prep schools in Butte.

Gary Turner said it was inevitable I'd meet someone like Holden. "You're going to leave Butte, right?" he said. "Right?" Gary Turner hobbled with a limp that made him seem, at the time to the most of us, a touch prissy. It was polio. Why he caught polio while the rest of us didn't who dared say? We'd all swum in the same public pool: a huge concrete thing in Clark Park built by Anaconda Copper along with a ball field, a skating rink, teeter-totters, slides, swings, and sunken pit trampolines that were filled in when Robby Brunnell broke his neck and was paralyzed from his jawbone down.

I haven't seen Gary in forty years. At some point I was told he'd married a dancer, had studied dance history, and was teaching choreography somewhere in Utah or Arizona. Nevada perhaps. His wife was of the exotic sort: Apache or Basque. I don't get to Butte much now. Gary's brother Teddy doesn't live there anymore and both their parents are dead. Anyway, I don't get home much, if you want to know. I see Knievel's kid on a Harley jumping buses on TV. It seems like I read where Evel had his house confiscated for back taxes and how he was sued by someone because he'd hit him with a bat, an aluminum bat or some such. Do I know for sure? No. But I hear rumors.

Gary Turner once asked me to his house after school. To tell the truth, I was better friends with his brother Teddy, but I went. It was the year Gary was a senior and I was junior in high school: 1962 — the year before Gary left for Snow. He'd asked me to his house to play a record. The record Gary played was *Sketches of Spain* which, I now know, had been recorded by Miles Davis just the year before. The first black man I saw was on TV. There were no blacks in the mines in Butte. There were Irish, Czechs, Finns, Italians, Jews, Hispanics, Chinese, Filipinos, Crow Indians, but no blacks. Gary danced a little to Davis's good music with his leg in that brace.

I guess I should point out that I did leave Butte. I've lived in France and Belgium and Luxembourg. I've worked in Washington, D.C. I have a degree from Cornell. I've run into preppies, which has made my move back west a fresh breeze. I'm considering a leave of absence from work to drive about and to look for deaf-mutes. I'm serious — let me say it: I reread the book, and I'm on the lookout again for H. C. Rereading the book reminded me. It reminded me, too, of Gary and Evel and Evel's brother who slipped in the shaft at the mine. And of my own father who is dead. And of my brother, seven years younger who has died, whose wife I've not bothered to call. And of my other brother who's even younger and gay and who, with his partner, stole the family home from my mother who remarried three months after my father died and of my sister who was barren then adopted a child and then dropped ten or eleven more with her husband (natural birth somewhere in Kentucky) and of my adopted Shoshone sister who sleeps with radio disc jockeys and then sells the births to couples who are flush attorneys or of my oldest sister who with her husband has lived in a trailer all their lives on property they early paid for and then built a garage four times the square footage of their tin home for their four-wheel drives and canoes and freezers. *It's funny. Don't ever tell anybody anything. If you do, you start missing everybody.* But you know that.

Donald Anderson

P.S. Lightning struck the house today and fried the garage door opener again. Here on the mesa, across the street though, this same lightning struck a neighbor. His name is Fred Mix — Frederick Mix. The police accident report reported unspecified neurological damage. It is a form report his wife showed me. In the section where it asks if weather was a factor, the police officer wrote *Yes*.

❦   Donald Anderson's story collection *Fire Road* won Iowa's 2001 John Simmons Short Fiction Award. He lives in Colorado.

Dear J. D. Salinger,

One of my clearest, happiest memories is of myself at fourteen, sitting up in bed, being handed a large glass of warm buttermilk by my mother because I had a sore throat, and she saying how jealous she was that I was reading *The Catcher in the Rye* for the first time. As have so many other unpopular, oversensitive American teenagers over the last fifty years, I memorized the crucial passages of the novel and carried it around with me wherever I went. The following year, my older sister said that *Catcher* was good, very good in its own way, but that it was really time to move on now to *Nine Stories*, so I did. My identification with Seymour in "A Perfect Day for Bananafish" was extreme enough that my mother scheduled a few sessions for me with a psychologist-friend of hers, and "For Esmé — with Love and Squalor" remains one of my favorite stories ever written. In college, I judged every potential girlfriend according to how well she measured up to Franny in *Franny and Zooey*. In graduate school, under the influence of *Raise High the Roof Beam, Carpenters* and *Seymour: An Introduction*, I got so comma-, italics-, and parenthesis-happy one semester that my pages bore less resemblance to prose fiction than to a sort of newfangled Morse code.

When I can't sleep, I get up and pull a book off the shelf. There are fewer than ten writers whom I can reliably turn to in this situation and you are one of them. I've read each of your books at least a dozen times. What is it in your work that offers such solace of the soul at three A.M.? For me, it's how your voice, to a different degree and in a different way in every book, talks back to itself, how it listens to itself talking, comments upon what it hears, and keeps talking. This self-awareness, this self-reflexiveness is the pleasure and burden of being conscious, and the gift of your work — what makes me less lonely and makes life more livable — lies in its revelation that this isn't a deformation in how I think; this is how human beings think. Thank you.

Sincerely,
David Shields

🦋   David Shields's book *Black Planet: Facing Race during an NBA Season* was a finalist for the National Book Critics Circle Award. His new book, *Enough about You: Adventures in Autobiography*, was recently published by Simon & Schuster.

Dear Mr. Salinger,

Like almost everyone else, I first read *Catcher* in the Rye in school, on a lazy afternoon, the books passed down from the front, encouragingly slim under their maroon covers. We were the advanced class, battle-hardened veterans of *Julius Caesar* and *Silas Marner,* used to Literature with the capital "L." Literature with the capital "L" was good for us like castor oil and mixed vegetables, and would help us get into good colleges. The meek may or may not inherit the earth, but the suburban meek with excellent SAT scores could get a jump on the rabble. So I opened *The Catcher in the Rye,* hunkered down to see what the damage might be, and the rest of the world melted away.

Here was the first time I connected to a character: someone who felt out of place, who yearned to escape, but didn't know what from. For the first time I thought that fiction (small "f" which also included farting, fighting, and fucking — two out of three at that stage, but I had ambitions) might be that method of escape. Fiction could be about people I knew and things I thought and cared about. Holden was funny and real and shouted out loud the confusion none of us had dared to whisper. It's not too much to say that in reading Holden's coming-of-age story I came of age.

Now I have my own son, James, a good boy like I once was, but one who thinks of reading as manual labor for the eyes. He had some ditch-digging to do.

"How about *The Catcher in the Rye,*" I said, picking up a copy.

"What's it about?" he asked, his face clouding with suspicion.

"Just listen," I said, opening to the first page, and began to read.

People wonder about your silence, as if you owed us something, but it's just because we miss Holden, and miss the part of ourselves that was Holden, the part of ourselves that held out against the phonies before we joined their too orderly ranks, the part of ourselves that could read a piece of fiction and think: *my life will never be the same.*

So let me just finish by saying this: you don't owe us; we owe you, and this is a way, however inadequate, of saying thanks.

All best,
Robert O'Connor

❦ Robert O'Connor is the author of the novel *Buffalo Soldiers* and was named one of the Best Young American Novelists by *Granta*. He teaches at Oswego State University.

Dear Mr. Salinger:

When I think of you, I think first of *The Catcher in the Rye*. Proust tells us that the books we love always remain (or is it always should remain?) in our minds, if not actually in our possession, in the copies in which we first read them. I first read a paperback edition of *Catcher*. I forget the publisher (Avon? Pocket books?) and the price (25 cents?), but I clearly remember the shiny cover, which depicts a realistic, almost photographed looking Holden Caulfield, tall and stern in profile, wearing his hunting hat. He's standing on a city street and looks a bit too much like a movie poster of the period, just as the haggard but sexy Winston Smith on the cover of 1984 around the same time looks more heroic than Orwell probably intended.

This paperback lived in my older sister's room, a tiny oblong, halfway down the long, dark, winding hall of our ground-floor apartment, that had originally been intended to be a maid's room. In her glassed-in bookcase were many enticing books. What come to mind now are paperbacks of *Cat on a Hot Tin Roof, Measure for Measure,* and Henry Miller's *Sexus.* Why these three? Because the kinds of words I was learning from *The Catcher in the Rye* turned up in them as well: "lech" or "whore," for example, though probably only *Catcher* was a source of "fart."

These other books I flipped around in at the age of nine or ten, enjoying, for example, the photographs of Elizabeth Taylor in a slip and Paul Newman in pajamas in *Cat*. But *The Catcher in the Rye* I inhaled.

In those days, it came naturally to me to memorize, more or less, the books I liked, since the books I liked, I read over and over. My many early readings of *Catcher* blur and merge in my mind, but they or their composite remain vivid when I open the book today and realize I know it nearly by heart, italics and all. And the same is true of the *Nine Stories*. "Olives and wax — I never go anywhere without 'em." "You take a really sleepy man, Esmé . . ."

The summer I was ten or so, I had a tiny part in William Saroyan's play *The Time of Your Life* when the play was performed at Bread Loaf. I played the bartender's daughter (my line was a proud "That's my father"), and I must have spent a lot of time listening to rehearsals or, on stage, hanging around the bar, because some of the lines spoken by other characters remain so vivid to me. Kitty, a prostitute, says to some man who's annoying her, "I'm a whore, you son of a bitch. You know what I do. And I know what you do." It's hard to believe in 2000, but that line was raunchy fare for an innocent little girl around 1958. I did and didn't understand what it meant.

And something like the same doubleness clings to my memory of these early encounters with you, Mr. Salinger. I learned new words, and understood, more or less, what they meant. But what the books had to say to me was not merely a matter of whores and farts. There was a very different message, if that's the word, intertwined with the bravado, the scenes of New York at night, the loneliness and disillusionment. Peel back Holden's unease and indignation, his desire to expose the phony world of grownups; peel back the bellhop, the prostitute, Ackley; and the atmosphere that rises from *The Catcher in the Rye* turns out, for me at least, to be one of kindness, comfort, patience, and safety. These qualities reside not so much in the world of the book (though they can be found there if you look), but in its language; in the voice of the narrator. Of course this voice takes the form, in *Catcher*, of Holden's voice; but a similar if not identical wryness, sense of detail, and overall alertness to the gamut of human behavior can be heard in the voice of "A Perfect Day for Bananafish," "Down at the Dinghy," "For Esmé — with Love and Squalor" — the list goes on. The squalor, in other words, is always being balanced by love.

Last summer, teaching at the Sewanee Writers Conference, I and my family spent twelve days in a borrowed faculty house on campus. It was a nice little house, its upstairs still undergoing renovation, and I love Sewanee, where I had taught several other summers. But these nearly two weeks were an uncomfortable period. Many people at the conference, including me, came down with vicious colds which weren't improved by the contrast between the unremitting heat outside and the refrigerated temperatures of the air-conditioning inside. My husband came down with the cold and was quite sick. Our fifteen-year-old son and the friend he had brought along for solidarity slept till noon every day and prowled, or slunk, around the campus the rest of the time, spending hours at the local coffee shop and disappearing into the dorm rooms of new, glamorously older undergraduate or townie friends, from whom they picked up anti-gown attitudes. Superimpose on this a strenuous schedule of workshops, conferences, readings, more readings, endless literary conversations. I could hardly wait for this hot and cold interlude to end.

But the time was significantly improved when I came upon a copy of *Raise High the Roof Beam, Carpenters* on our hosts' bookshelves. There it all was: the heat, the sense of time stretching out endlessly, the being jammed together in space and time with other equally uncomfortable people. Not having first read *Carpenters* as a nine year-old (perhaps I'd been fifteen), I'd forgotten how hilarious the story of Seymour's abortive wedding and that endless traffic jam was. More squalor than love this time around, perhaps. But again, peel back the Matron of Honor and the taxi driver and the tiny deaf-mute uncle and the words Boo Boo has scrawled in soap on the mirror, and there is an enormous and consoling patience in the telling. Reading about that boiling hot nonwedding made the shivery, sweaty, sneezy, achy, teen-age ridden time in that little house into something I could begin to assimilate. It reminded me of my love of reading. It was an escape and a refuge. It even made me homesick for Manhattan.

I could go on, but this is probably more than enough. Thank you, Mr. Salinger. It's easy to say that I will never forget your books; but it's also true that I have forgotten scarcely a word you've written.

Your fan,
Rachel Hadas

Rachel Hadas teaches English at the Newark campus of Rutgers University and is the author of more than a dozen books of poetry, essays, and translations. Her new book of poems is called *Indelible*.

Dear J. D.—

I'm sorry this letter has taken me so long. I started it back in September, 2000, on my father's birthday when I was thinking about Allie's fielder's mitt, the one for left-handers with the poems in green ink all over the fingers and pocket.

I used to play right field as a kid and I think that's when I became a poet, standing out there in the green grass and sunlight waiting for something to happen — waiting a hell of a long time — and when something did happen, a white ball floating all dreamlike in the air toward me, I wasn't ready for it. But I guess that's how life is — you're never really ready for the changes.

Anyway, I keep thinking of Allie's glove because when my sister called three years ago, all hysterical, and said my father died in his sleep, I just walked down to the basement and found my old Rawlings glove and remembered how I would oil it and keep a baseball tied up in it. But what I remember most is how before we'd play catch my father would rub his hand through his hair then rub that hand into the palm of the mitt where he would spit, then pound his fist, over and over, then he'd give me the glove back and we'd play catch.

But the day my father died I went down to the basement, turned off the light and just stuck my nose in that mitt like a dog and smelled and smelled my father there, just like I used to smell the inside of his hats when I was a kid, and I never wanted to take my nose out of that glove where our sweaty smells were all good and mixed up in the dark.

Mark Irwin

✤   Mark Irwin's fourth collection of poetry, *White City*, was recently nominated for the National Book Critics Circle Award. He spends part of each year on a wilderness ranch in Colorado.

Dear J. D.:

First of all, let's establish that I don't want anything from you. Not an interview, or a relic, or an autograph. Naturally, I'd be pleased to receive an acknowledgment . . . but I don't really expect one. So, it is *I* who want to give something to *you* — something you may not even want — and it will be satisfaction enough for me simply to know that I have done so.

I have wanted to write you, to share this family anecdote, for some years; always, I have hesitated out of a combined respect for your privacy and fear of rebuff. Suddenly, I have realized neither of these are really valid reasons for not writing. You and I are the only players in the following dialog who remain alive, so I feel compelled somehow to share it with you. Doing so is my business: whether and how you elect to receive it is yours.

It's a simple enough story. And I've enclosed a little diagram showing how the people interrelate. The confusion is right out of classical humor . . . but funny only to those aware of the people, their relationships, occupations, residences, and nicknames.

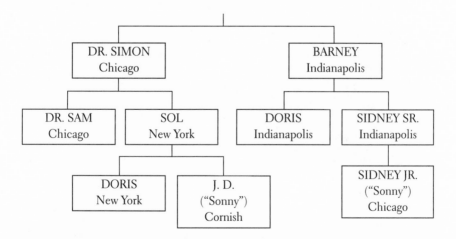

The conversation took place, as closely as I can pinpoint it, in about 1949. I was sixteen, and living in Chicago. My grandfather, Barney Salinger, was in Chicago, visiting his brother, Simon (your grandfather). Your father, Sol, was there, visiting his father, as well. Simon was living in a downtown residence hotel, the Maryland; one afternoon, after school, I decided to phone my grandfather there. Your father answered the phone; the following conversation, as nearly as I can remember it, ensued:

"Hello?"

"Is Mr. Salinger there?"

"This is Mr. Salinger."

"No, I wanted to speak to the doctor's brother."

"I *am* the doctor's brother. Who do you want?"

"Uh — Doris's father?"

"Yes, this is Doris's father. Who is this?"

"This is Sonny."

"C'mon, now young man. Who *is* this calling?"

"Honest — this is Sidney. Sidney Salinger."

"Sidney?! What are *you* doing in town?"

"I *live* here. Who is *this?*"

Finally, your dad and I got things untangled. I don't know if he ever thought about the phone conversation again, but I've remembered it for years. My father and Aunt Doris always got a bang out of it. A true "comedy of errors" — funny only to "insiders."

Best regards,
Sid Salinger, Jr.

🦋 Sid Salinger, now retired, resides in Sun City Roseville, California. Sid and J. D. Salinger are second cousins.

Dear J. D. Salinger:

I was always looking for you. In the fall of 1967 I went to Vermont to teach English at Windsor High School. Larry Taylor who taught senior English told me about how you used to sit in the back of his classroom and hang out with the kids. Larry said, "I know Jerry very well."

My landlady Mrs. Barrows told me about how you came up to her in the Super Duper in the early '50s and asked if you could buy her a cup of coffee. At Nap's Lunch you asked her what it was like to live around Windsor because you were thinking of moving up from New York City. Mrs. Barrows was an LPN and very often when your kids were sick you would have her up to spend the night. She said, "Old Sal, he's a good guy."

I learned that even though you lived in New Hampshire, you picked up your mail in Windsor. I never saw you at the post office. I found out that the school paper was the only paper you had ever given an interview to. I never saw you at the school. The kids told me you talked to them, but you didn't talk to adults because they would go around telling everybody they had talked to you.

I was twenty-two and had never seen a real writer, particularly one whose books I liked. I wanted to be — and in the way of young people even assumed I would become — Buddy Glass someday. So I looked for you always in the Dartmouth Library, the Bookstore, the streets of Hanover and Windsor. But you weren't there.

Another young teacher and her husband were hiking the Dartmouth trails when she sprained her ankle. Her husband went down the mountain to get help. She sat alone for a bit and then a guy appeared out of the woods. He asked if he could help and then said he would stay until her husband got back. They had a nice talk about the weather and the fall until he saw her husband returning with help, and then abruptly said goodbye. The medic said, "Salinger usually doesn't talk to people."

In June of 1972 I decided to return to the Midwest. I was living in Wood-stock then and the night before I left I took one last walk around. I stopped to look over an old desk in the window of an antique store. I felt a presence behind me and looked up at the reflection in the window and it was you. I looked right into the reflection's eyes with a shock of recognition and you looked right into my eyes and nodded, Yes, and then shook your head, No. I waited until you walked down the street before I turned around.

So I never did talk to you. It is just as well. What would I have said?

Dex Westrum

❦   Dex Westrum has published books, stories, essays, radio plays, and educational films. He teaches writing and film at Upper Iowa University in Milwaukee, Wisconsin.

Dear Mr. Salinger,

I was fortunate to have known Marilyn Monroe from the late '50s until her death in 1962. I attended her private method acting classes where she was assisted by her acting tutor, Paula Strasberg, and fellow-actor, George Peppard.

Marilyn had decided to change her image and develop as a producer and director in the hopes of reviving her "Marilyn Monroe Productions" company and establishing her own Studio-College and campus town. She lacked the self-confidence to share her own dream with most of her peers, fearing ridicule and disdain, but convinced herself that by teaching children in her spare time she could build both a portfolio and gain that confidence she sorely lacked. After all, she adored children and their love for her was easily reciprocated.

I was the first child recruited at the tender age of seven years old. Marilyn and Paula began allowing me to write scripts for use in their acting workshops. I continued writing for them over the next four years. They began by teaching me the simple rules of grammar and syntax, and gradually they introduced me to writing simple sentences, paragraphs, outlines, short stories, and eventually taught me the format of script writing. In addition, they had me research various authors and they taught me their influence on our culture.

Marilyn introduced me to Holden Caulfield and Seymour in 1961. The world would be surprised to know how well read she was. Marilyn spoke highly of several writers including Norman Mailer, Truman Capote, and you, J. D. Salinger. What she lacked in a formal education she more than made up for in self-determination and intense study. We often researched and shared books together. I was a witness to her determination to improve herself.

Marilyn had read *Catcher* and "A Perfect Day for Bananafish" so thoroughly that she was able to conduct a lecture of quite a few minutes in duration without the benefit of notes. She attempted to draw comparisons between Holden and Seymour. Unfortunately, the Marilyn workshops (as with the Strasberg Actors Studio in New York) did not permit the audio or video recording of those sessions, and after forty years the memory has somewhat faded, but I have managed to retain the essence of that lecture, and I can assure you it was inspired. Marilyn discussed with me her feelings about Holden's concern for "phonies" and Seymour's perfect day for killing himself. However, before one might draw the conclusion that Marilyn's supposed own perfect day of self-destruction was somehow influenced by Seymour's action, I would disagree. Marilyn stressed to me, as late as 1962, only some two months before her death, the importance of life, and the responsibility of us all to catch and keep others from going over the cliff.

Mr. Salinger, it was your stories and the world of TV and films in the hands of Marilyn Monroe that inspired me to continue writing long after Marilyn's death. Years later I would use the analytical and writing skills I acquired in those workshops to be an Intelligence Analyst for the CIA, Social Service Program Specialist for HEW, a Computer Specialist/Programmer-Analyst for the Federal Government, a song writer, and a certified Public Access Cable TV Producer, Writer, and Director.

I respect your privacy and I'm writing this not to be read by you, but by all the Holden Caulfields and Seymours who reject the phony world and search for their perfect day with the Bananafish.

> *Respectfully,*
> *Robert Surface*

🦋 Robert Surface took acting classes from Marilyn Monroe and was involved with Marilyn in intelligence courier work for the Kennedy administration. He has worked for the CIA and FBI and now works for the Department of Justice.

Dear J. D. Salinger:

I made you a character in my 1982 novel *Shoeless Joe* because over the years you have made yourself conspicuous by hiding, claiming not to want publicity but raising hell every time someone mentions your name in the media. I also knew you had worked your way through college as an actor on a cruise ship, therefore you know how to hold an audience, and have done so many years without any new publications. Reading your collected and uncollected stories I found you had used two characters named Kinsella, Ray in "A Young Girl in 1941 with No Waist at All," published in *Mademoiselle*, and Richard in *The Catcher in the Rye*: those were the connections I needed to draw you into my world of otherworldly baseball. Kinsella is an uncommon name, so I would name my character Ray Kinsella and have him turn up on your doorstep saying, "I'm one of your fictional characters come to life." Years later I received a letter from a Kinsella in Massachusetts who had been your college roommate, so one small mystery was solved. When my book appeared my publisher's lawyers received a grumbling letter from your attorneys saying that you were outraged and offended to be portrayed as a character in my book, and that you would be very unhappy if the work were transferred to other media. Hollywood didn't have the balls to use you as a character in the movie *Field of Dreams*, opting instead for a generic black reclusive author that you couldn't claim was a thinly disguised you. My publisher's lawyers said to me, "Look, all he can sue us for is about the sixth definition of libel called 'false light' in which case he would have to go to court and say, 'I've been portrayed in this book as a kindly, loving, humorous individual, while in reality I am a surly so-and-so who occasionally shoots at tourists when they drive by my house, therefore I've been portrayed in a false light.'" I'm not sorry that I did what I did and I hope that over the years you've come to enjoy my wise and warm portrayal of you.

> *Go the distance,*
> *Bill Kinsella*

❦

❦   W. P. Kinsella is the author of many novels including *Shoeless Joe, The Iowa Baseball Confederacy,* and *Go the Distance: Baseball Stories.*

PART TWO

Students & Teachers

"You'll learn from them—if you want to. Just as someday, if you have something to offer, someone will learn something from you. It's a beautiful reciprocal arrangement. And it isn't education. It's history. It's poetry."

— J. D. Salinger, *The Catcher in the Rye*

Dear Neighbor,

Even though you live high up on the hills with a view across the river and famous covered bridge to Mount Ascutney, while I am moving in on the Flat with the traffic between Claremont and Hanover rumbling by, I feel that we should think of ourselves as neighbors. There are no more people in the town of Cornish than in some single New York City apartment houses and since we share the right to speak at the same town meeting about mutual concerns should we wish, it seems civil to offer you my greetings.

I imagine that some of our neighbors — and perhaps even you — will feel that because I did write an introductory book about your fiction for a new series on many American authors, I have moved up here just to try to break in on your privacy; but I didn't. After spending three years trying to establish a Department of English at a new state university in Indianapolis, I felt that I needed a secluded place myself to get on with some of my own writing. I came to this area because one of my best former students had just competed successfully for a trial appointment at Dartmouth, and I wanted to be near someone that I felt I could depend upon in this unfamiliar region. I was also attracted here because my father's family had lived here for several generations in New Hampshire before migrating westward. At fifty, I thought it was time to become acquainted with ancestral country. I settled first, however, across the Connecticut River in Vermont; but, after a year, I decided that I'd like to buy a summer residence here. When spring thaw came, I started inspecting places around Lake Mascoma. I never even thought about Cornish. Even after a year living nearby, I still didn't even know how to get here. I ended up in the hills on a back road with my Volkswagen stuck in the mud. Undaunted, I finally found the connecting road to the Flat and a modified Greek revival house (c. 1830), as those with a room overhanging the front porch are called. I liked its possibilities for restoration and bought it. After redecorating the interior, I moved in with my aging mother.

Not that I wouldn't like to get to know you, as I would all my neighbors, most of whom I have met; but not so that I could pester you with questions about what your stories *mean* or your private American Dream or even why such a long delay in getting another new story into the *New Yorker*, but because I've heard from Blair Watson, who runs the film program at Dartmouth, that you collect old movies and used to come up there to some of their programs until people started recognizing you. I collect films, too; and I thought we might both enjoy some exchanges. We wouldn't even have to meet. We could just exchange lists and reels through some neutral ground like town clerk Berenice Fitch's office or the Powers store near my house. I imagine you have many more 16mm prints than I've been able to collect; but I have some uncommon items like early Technicolor experiments and Orson Welles's first short. On the other hand, though, I recognized that you might not even want strangers looking at your prints, because, like the boy in Holden Caulfield's favorite story by his now-Hollywood-prostituted brother, "The Secret Goldfish," you didn't want anyone else to see your prize possessions because you had bought them with your own money. I hope you're still enjoying happy viewing anyway.

> *Enjoy yourself as you have given others enjoyment,*
> *Warren French*

✖ Warren French published the first book-length study of Salinger in 1963. He has also written critical texts on the writings of John Steinbeck and Frank Norris.

Dear Mr. Salinger:

As in many other schools across the country, *The Catcher in the Rye* was required reading in my high school in the early 1980s. Teachers assumed that we would identify with Holden Caulfield and his general distrust of all things adult, and, for the most part, they were correct. Holden cut an attractive figure: a bit transgressive, a bit of a truth-sayer, a bit of a punk. We all wanted to tell it like it is. We knew.

But I've got a secret about what I knew. Three-quarters of the way through the book, I stopped identifying with Holden and became much more intrigued with a character whose fictional life spans only a handful of pages — Mr. Antolini. I'm sure you remember the scene. Holden, looking for comfort in a world seemingly intent on dispelling all of his cherished delusions, returns to his favorite former English teacher and spends the night at his place. We all understand the scene. We return in times of heartache and trouble to the places of comfort, of refuge — to what we know, or think we know.

Holden awakens to find Antolini stroking his head. The boy freaks and quickly leaves.

In McCarthy America, with its rampant, sanctioned queer-baiting and homophobia, you must have known how Antolini would have been read. What else could he have been but the faggot teacher molesting his student? And this is how Holden sees him. And this is how Holden becomes — for me, at least — less the critic of his age than its product.

But there are so many other ways to read this encounter. For me, this brief scene offered one of the very few glimpses into male-male affection that I had ever seen in literature up to that point. As an adolescent just coming into consciousness of my own interest in male bodies, I hardly thought of Antolini as a monster. He was downright intriguing. Indeed, even at fifteen, a sophomore in high school, I wondered why Holden ran away from Antolini. I might have stayed — certainly bothered a bit by the questions forming themselves as a hollow in my gut, but more and more interested in the origin of the teacher's caress. To be frank, I don't think much would have passed between us, besides a smile. Then a handshake and goodbye.

But what would I have left with? And what does Holden flee from?

We cannot know what Mr. Antolini's intentions were. His story is only given to us in parts most easy to misread, most open to malignant interpretation. But for me, Antolini held out the possibility of adult sexuality, of tenderness between men, and of intimacy forbidden. It may be that Holden, protector of innocence, must flee this adult world. But in fleeing, he closes the door on a character that some of us needed to know more about. Some of us were looking for our own Antolinis, and Holden's callous rejection seems cruel. At best, it passes a judgment on a character whose intentions are never revealed. At worst, it shows Holden to be a bigot.

And this is the point where I stopped identifying with Holden, where I stopped trusting what he had to say about the world.

Ultimately, though, this is not just a problem of reading a (potentially) queer character. For me, as a queer teacher, this is a problem of pedagogy in its broadest — and most intimate — implications. Let me explain with my own story.

Once, one of my dearest friends and colleagues couldn't wait to tell me the news. Another victory, albeit small, had been scored in the struggle for toleration of homosexuals. And apparently, unbeknownst to me, I was directly involved. The story is simple enough and even seemingly innocuous.

The scene is that of a small western university where I was one of only two openly gay teachers. The time is late one afternoon, after my building's main office had been closed for the day. Going to check my mail, I happenstanced upon a student frantically trying to get into the office to place an essay into his professor's mailbox. The student, seeing his opportunity, asked if I would let him in so he could turn his paper in and avoid a late grade. I was delighted to do so, giving him a hearty "you're welcome" to his obviously grateful "thanks."

I then completely forgot this incident.

That is, I completely forgot this incident until my colleague explained to me the next day how I had transformed this young man's understanding of homosexuals. You see, this man was one of my colleague's most troubling students, an individual who, in a gender studies course, was often very resistant to exploring the intricacies of sexism and heterosexism, an individual who couldn't comprehend the ongoing battles that women and gays face in their struggle for acknowledgment and acceptance. In this one particular case, however, and for this one individual man, I had made a difference. The student confided in my colleague that my kindness to him had made him think that I must be a "good guy," and, even though homosexual, I was really "OK" and "nice after all."

I couldn't believe what I was hearing. Me, a good guy? Nice and OK? For this student, and my colleague, yes; I was helping to save the day and alter, one individual at a time, the course of bigotry as it pulses through and poisons all of our lives.

But an irony lurks here, perhaps one that Mr. Antolini could understand. Certainly, I was happy to help the student — just another day at the office for any teacher, really. We would do the same for anyone. But I must admit that my attention to this young man, the heartiness of my response, my own eagerness to be of assistance was laced through and through with a faint attraction for this good-looking boy. And while I would have assisted anyone in a similar predicament, I think my queerness, my appreciation for an attractive young man, made my willingness to help seem all the more friendly, all the more "nice after all."

Of course, as soon as I admit this, I fear some will think their worst fears corroborated. See? The faggot teacher preying on his students. But that's not the full story is it? As with Mr. Antolini's little scene, you see the caress. You may even guess what motivates it. Then most are quickly overwhelmed, like Holden, by their fears, their interpretations. But that's their story.

I have become Mr. Antolini. And I can at least thank you, Mr. Salinger, for this early, tender glimpse into the kind of teacher that I wanted — and that I want to continue to be.

Jonathan Alexander

Jonathan Alexander is an assistant professor of English and women's studies at the University of Cincinnati, where he teaches writing, lesbian and gay studies, and Web literacy.

Dear J. D. Salinger:

In 1976, the editor of a scholarly magazine, knowing I was a fan of yours, asked me to write an article: *"The Catcher in the Rye* after Twenty-Five Years."* I accepted eagerly. I was immersed in Eastern philosophy and religion and this seemed an inspired opportunity to read the articles on *Catcher* and your other books and to enjoy the learned discussions on Buddhist, Hindu, and Taoist ideas and practices which are so central to your work.

But what a surprise! There were no such articles. I could hardly locate any serious discussion of Eastern thought in twenty-five years of Salinger criticism. There was an occasional reference to it in passing, often in simplified, third-hand terms, usually with a hint of embarrassment, treated like the drunken uncle who appears out of the attic during a respectable tea party. Most of the articles were by East Coast critics who faced toward Europe. Though in many cases they liked your work, most didn't seem to understand what you were wrestling with.

I saw here, clearly, the ignorance you had been facing when you published your writing, and how lonely it must have made you feel. In a sense, you already were isolated in a kind of New Hampshire before you moved there. I changed my article into one about the influence of Eastern thought on your work and then expanded it into a small book, *Zen in the Art of J. D. Salinger,* which opened a new field in Salinger study. It sold out two printings but then the publisher went into hibernation and now the book has been out of print for twenty years. "So it goes," as one of your Army colleagues, also shocked by World War II, would say.

Some of the points I made in the book might interest you. Holden's story follows the story of the Buddha. A privileged young man comes into contact with sickness and old age (Mr. Spencer), and death (his brother Allie), and sets off on a journey outside his protected world to try to find meaning in this newly discovered territory beyond innocence. Seeing this archetypal narrative in *Catcher* made me realize the universality of the Buddha's story. It is a primary story about the mortality that all good authors must confront in their lives and should confront in their works.

I suggested that in *Franny and Zooey* the identity of the mysterious Fat Lady points toward Bessie, the mother of the quiz kids who performs good works, serving Franny chicken soup, while all her children are engaged in esoteric philosophical speculations. Zooey actually calls his mother "Fatty" twice, even though she isn't fat.

Holden is "holdin" on to Allie's baseball glove, as a way of not letting go of Allie. His journey is a search for the meaning of life in the face of the black hole of Allie's death. Yet no adult he meets can answer his questions. Holden is learning that our modern Scientific-Enlightenment culture is virtually unique in the history of the world in not providing answers or myths for our fears about dying, nor methods to live with the sad knowledge that our lives and the world are ephemeral. This is, of course, the first law of the Buddha — life is suffering, but the Buddha also promises there is an answer to the problem of suffering and it was your courage and genius to set off in search of a solution.

Catcher, like *The Adventures of Huckleberry Finn,* is a radical book. The people who tried to ban them were wrong in their response, but they were correct in their analysis of what the books were saying. These are not innocent stories for kids. I've always said that American society is a hurdle race in which you have to run *under* the hurdles. Both *Catcher* and *Huck Finn* present America as a lost world in which there is no way for a youngster to become an independent, feeling, knowledgeable adult. Twain in *The Mysterious Stranger* came so close to an answer, seeing the world as a dream, but this vision left him depressed and mystified. He couldn't take the next step, engaging with Eastern philosophies that accept and include the premise that the world is an illusion. As the Zen Masters say, we can get you to the top of a fifty-foot pole but we can't make you jump.

I grew up in the Bronx in a house without books. But when I did discover books, two American authors touched my life in a special way: You and Jack Kerouac. It wasn't until years later that I realized you two were introducing Eastern thought to the American novel. You didn't stop with fashionable despair. You went beyond the critics and the professors, beyond the liberal middle-class intellectual culture and you both paid the price for it. Interestingly, *both* of you wound up in isolation, far from the center of this subculture, the New York City publishing world. (Kerouac finally married his high school girlfriend and they moved to a nondescript house in St. Petersburg, Florida, living an anonymous, French Canadian, working class, retired life.)

It is no accident that you and Kerouac were among the favorites of the sixties generation, which was quite willing to move beyond the bounds of the conventionally accepted view of reality. Something significant and beautiful did happen in the sixties. Philip Roth and Woody Allen didn't understand this, and their works, though brilliant in their ways, are limited. They used their fame and ability to move up in the culture, right toward the center, to Manhattan, to the top of the high-culture world. But somehow you saw the dead end. You *began* at Park Avenue and the Stork Club. You understood that the visions of both the no-brain right wingers and the culture-accumulating sophisticates were bankrupt.

Tolstoy had seen this. That's why he stopped writing fiction after *Anna Karenina*. He said he wasn't going to spend his life entertaining the bourgeoisie. He moved to the country, built a school for the peasants and turned to religious matters. And Dostoyevsky saw it as well. These are the kind of writers you turned me on to. Those who attacked the questions of death and meaning head-on. You were my first real teacher. And thus, like any good student, I must now rebel a bit.

I read the books written about you by Joyce Maynard and your daughter. No doubt these accounts are informed and biased by the anger of the writers. (You do have the power to evoke passion in those who want to love you. Witness this present letter of mine.) Yet they are both recklessly courageous books in their way, confronting the old lion in his den, and Joyce has backed into writing a very interesting book.

Both books corroborate each other in the picture of you they present: A man who is deeply dedicated to his work, who is living in his books, devoting his life to them. Yet they also portray you as a man who has become confused about his values. For it turns out that you supported the Vietnam War. You loathed the hippies and mind-expanding drugs (the sacred plants of other cultures) and the antiwar movement. You don't like most black music — rock, and rhythm and blues, and progressive jazz — and, in the days before VHS, you spent much of your free time projecting films you had purchased, viewing again and again the thirties and forties movies of your youth and watching Lawrence Welk on the television.

You were not involved in what was happening. You got your news from corporate sources — the New York Times and TV. You moved to the whitest state in the union and, in many of your opinions and tastes, you joined the other privileged people whose expertise and power lay in the old view of those scientists and straight professors who had replaced the Church as the source of reasoning to lock up would-be Galileos and stop the young people who turned to the new technology of their time — the sacred medicines — and saw planets that couldn't be seen with the naked eye.

Somehow your picture of the sixties became that of the other straight white males of your generation. Had you forgotten just what it was about the Army that drove you nuts, that deadly melding of self-righteousness, hi-tech, and low consciousness that possesses all large modern armies, including our own, and that drove me crazy as well when I was a young company commander? How, in your view of the sixties, did you come to revert to the simplicity of those, like Philip Roth in American Pastoral, who had never experienced this?

Talk about projection!

The thinkers in the sixties caught on to the military-corporate-media-consumer complex that runs our culture. They caught on to the supposed "objectivity" of the *New York Times* and the scientific culture. Of course the sixties had to be stamped out. There was only so much money to be made in selling jeans and granola. New York, the great fifties city, had to reassert its cultural hegemony over cities like Ann Arbor, Cambridge, Austin, Madison, Seattle, Portland, Santa Fe, and dozens of others, most especially San Francisco, which faced Asia, not Europe, and was the capital of this new vision.

But we no longer live in the fifties. The theater center of New York today is not Broadway but Wall Street. This is the drama everyone is interested in. Broadway is a museum. The New York establishment art world is a branch of commerce and will someday be written about in books of business history.

And this is the old-culture worldview you chose. Maybe New Hampshire is not so far from Manhattan after all. Just a short drive in a new SUV.

The question that worries me is this: Can someone whose taste seems to have stopped about 1950, who gets his knowledge of the world largely through the *New York Times*, who idealizes an era when Duke Ellington could not stay in a hotel in much of the country, who prefers Lawrence Welk to John Coltrane, Monk, and the Temptations, can this person be the one who can translate the great eternal dharma of the Buddha and the Vedanta, the Hindus and the Tao into a language which is understandable and relevant to our time, here in the multicultural twenty-first century? Tolstoy and Dostoyevsky never danced the mashed potato, but they were a part of their own times; they understood what was happening in their country in their own lifetimes and were able to speak to their contemporaries about contemporary issues. The truth is in the details. Milarepa was silent in his cave, but he was not a country squire.

But enough of my squalor. Let's return to the love that inspired it. No one is perfect, not even the Pope or Gloria Steinem. Certainly not myself. Let me describe the moment when I first read *The Catcher in the Rye*.

The circumstances were certainly propitious. I was with my parents and brother driving from Montreal to the Thousand Islands. I was fourteen. My parents didn't read books. My grandparents were illiterate. My family was making a ten-day triangular summer trip from New York to Montreal to Toronto. For the rest of the summer we would swelter in our apartment in the concrete, pre–air conditioned Bronx. And this was when summers were summers — when people used to sleep on the fire escapes to get some air.

We never traveled. I didn't want to be on this trip. I wanted to be at summer camp, but my family had never been able to afford to send me there. My parents were looking out for our future. They had invested all our extra money in South Bronx real estate. My late grandfather had told them to buy apartment buildings. He said that even in a depression, people would always need a place to live. Unfortunately, he hadn't advised my parents about what to do when the tenants burned their own buildings down. But that was still a few years down the road.

My parents wanted me to understand that I had to put the family first and to enjoy the countryside. But I didn't understand. I was grumpy and self-ish. Besides, I didn't think I could appreciate nature very much. I knew it was probably OK in a way, like learning to speak Chinese, but having grown up in the bare streets of the Bronx, it was probably too late for me to begin. It would be like trying to appreciate opera, which to us meant liking the fat soprano from Akron, Ohio, who sang slightly off-key on the *Ted Mack Original Amateur Hour.*

I had never read a novel. I had started *Ivanhoe*, which had been assigned in junior high school, but this reinforced every prejudice against art that I grew up with. Books were for the rich. They were written in some strange language I could barely understand. They were about people with names like Rowena and knights in armor who called each other "thee" and "thou." What did this have to do with me? With Pin-Head Brady and his boys who tried to rob me every day on the way to school. With Miss O'Hare, the attendance officer, who had nabbed me for playing hooky for a month while going to the Museum of Natural History every day to see the dinosaurs. The dinosaurs were the only people I could identify with. They were obsolete. They couldn't make it in the modern world.

Mostly I worried about dying. One night my grandfather was gone. Poof! He wasn't even recently sick. Then the whole family fell apart. My grandmother started walking around in a befuddled trance and never spoke again. They had to get a nurse to care for her until she died. Then my unmarried aunt who lived with them began to sink. And my uncle Mac started to drink a quart of scotch a day and would call to taunt my father at night until my father would run out in his undershirt to kill him. Somehow we stopped my father as he strode toward the bar like a crazed zombie, walking down the middle of the street, wielding a hammer in the air over his head like a hatchet.

And there were all the other fights my father was getting into, attacking people over parking places, beating me up, trying to choke the neighbors; the only good note was that he usually lost.

And the mysteries of puberty arising. Or lack of puberty, which was worse.

Why were we here? How could the family have not prepared for the death of Grandpa? What was there in this crazy lethal world of Nazis and gangsters and idiotic violent kids that made life worth living at all?

But somehow, on our Canada trip, I bought a copy of *Catcher*. I don't know why. I guess it was the cover that attracted me. Maybe it was fate. In India they say your guru will show up when you are ready. Reading this book was like opening a door to a world in Technicolor. How could I come back to the world of black and white, the world that everyone I knew seemed to think was the only one there was?

As I lay on the motel bed near the Thousand Islands (the perfect location, on the border between two countries), my father said it was time to go on the boat tour. I said I would pass. He said I had to go. I said, I didn't want to go. I would stay home reading. He snapped and began to pummel me. Somehow I found myself running around the room with my father chasing me, trying to slug me. My mother screamed, "Sol! Sol! Not in his head! Don't hit his head!" My father was growling and swinging away. I ran into the closet, seized the doorknob, and held it. My father grabbed it from the other side and tried to twist it open. "Sol! Are you crazy!" my mother shrieked while my father shouted back as he struggled to get at me, "I paid a thousand bucks for this goddamn trip and that kid is going to see these goddamned islands if I have to kill him!"

Finally I relented. I knew that even if I stayed in the closet for a week, my father would still be there, twisting the knob and then he would *really* be angry. "I'll go," I said. "I'll see the islands."

My father relaxed. He had won by a decision, but it was still a victory. There was no reason to kill me. "You're goddamned right you'll see these goddamned islands," he said.

They *were* right, of course. I did like the islands. But when I returned to the motel, once again I walked through the door you had opened for me. The gateway into the world of literature.

It was you who showed me that books could be about me. That they could be honest, and written in a living language of the New York streets, that books could speak to my deepest questions of meaninglessness and death, helping me with the issues that seemed to be between me and the world at all times but which no one else seemed to notice. I now knew that there was at least one person in the world who understood what was bothering me, an adult who was sharp-sighted, smart, funny, and kind. For the first time in my life I had found a direction and a hope that there might be a reason to live. At the very least, I was no longer alone.

Thank you. Thank you so much more than I can say. I don't know what my life would have been like without you, but it wouldn't have been the same. You were my teacher, my doctor, my artist, and I was one of your perfect readers. When you studied homeopathy to free yourself from the one-dimensional model of traditional medicine, I understood. When you grew your own vegetables, and turned away from the world, I understood. When you used your fiction, with its vibrant characters and New York City street humor, and street compassion as a means for approaching the deepest philosophical issues of our lives, I understood. And when Joyce Maynard reported that the last time she saw you, in the midnineties, you told her that her problem was that she still loved life, I had to admit, reluctantly, that I understood that too.

When Ernest Becker wrote that we've built civilization as a way of denying the fact of death, I understood that, and I thought of you. But you hadn't stopped where Becker did, at the culture's conventional limits, a dignified stoicism, grin and bear it. If the definition of a hero is one who journeys outside the village fence into the dark, creature-filled woods and returns with knowledge that is a boon for his people, then you were a hero.

Yes, I began to understand. And later I also went into the woods. I was afraid of the woods, but somehow I went. Again and again. In the attack on the Pentagon in 1967, I stood up against the bayonets of the Army that had driven us both crazy. Later, I ate the Soma of the Upanishads, I sat under the Bo Tree with the Buddha, and I walked the road to Damascus. I saw the visions that were at the heart of all religions. When, in the *Bhagavad Gita,* Krishna revealed His awesome and terrifying godly Self to Arjuna, I understood, because Krishna had revealed His frightening magic and majesty to me as well.

I only wish you had been there too, if only in spirit. After all, what was the ending of *Catcher* if not Holden and Phoebe turning away from the hapless adults and toward each other, the young people beginning a counterculture?

But all this is a family quarrel, underpinned by love. I have always considered you my older brother. My actual brother, my younger brother Mark, was a top Wall Street lawyer. We had drifted apart some after I moved to

San Francisco but when he was dying of cancer at the age of forty-seven, he wanted to finish his life at his country home that I had never seen. I went with him up to Vermont and it was only when I got settled in there that I realized my brother was dying in the town in which you lived. Your house was across the bridge, on the New Hampshire side of the dividing stream, but this was your town. I didn't bother you of course, but as I walked around the town I did see where you buy your paper and etc., and I thought how strange life is. That my real brother, who didn't even know you lived there, had moved to the same town as my fictional brother and had chosen to die there.

Anyhow, I want to close now and to wish you well. This letter stirred up some old passions that I'm not sure I fully inhabit any longer. My wife and I live in a wonderful multicultural neighborhood where we lead a some-what reclusive life informed by a quiet spirituality. I've shed some of my anger and worldly ideals and have turned away from the noisy carnival to a degree, facing toward the healing Silence.

I used to think novels could change the world, now I'm not so sure. I do believe they can still touch the lives of certain people. If I'm alive when your next books come out, I'll be the first to read them. We have intelli-gent and well-written novels (and films) that describe the slow sinking of this titanic civilization. What we need are the kinds of stories you can tell, of what happens to people who have taken in too many of the culture's "bananas," people who feel themselves trapped, their souls endangered, but who have not given up and are still ransacking the underground his-tory of the world in search of a way out.

I know the power you have accrued by staying out of the light of celebrity which makes everyone look cheap. Many of us feel it. Some have said that a person of your gifts had an obligation to come down from the mountain and speak out in these dark and painful times, but in my opinion you've been speaking out loud and clear for fifty years. To paraphrase Henry Fonda at the end of the movie of *The Grapes of Wrath:* Whenever writers gather to take turns giving each other awards, you won't be there. Whenever writers show up at rich and fashionable parties to get their pictures in the magazines, you won't be there. Whenever writers stand in tuxedos at secular bar mitzvah–type events, whenever they appear in commercials, whenever they live beyond their means and have to do shoddy work to support their habits, whenever they make fools of themselves on television and wreck their own health and then have to turn their bodies over to the medical-pharmaceutical establishment, you won't be there.

I'll see you in heaven, Bro. Look for me in the Count Basie band. I'll be in the third sax chair. Emily Dickinson will be seated next to me in the second. The first, of course, will be reserved for the Prez.

With gratitude and love,
Gerald Rosen

✺ Gerald Rosen wrote *Zen in the Art of J. D. Salinger* and five novels including *The Carmen Miranda Memorial Flagpole.* He once played center-field with Willie Mays in the Polo Grounds.

Dear Mr. Salinger:

When I was eleven or twelve I was sent to the local library to do a research report, my first. This was forty-something years ago and branch libraries were still run by women with buns who shushed you, and who kept on the counter a list of books formally determined to be unfit to read. Such lists were invariably organized alphabetically and on this particular day your name was at the top just below a bold capital C. Like many boys that age of my era, I read only when I was made to, but I was also pubescent and I simply assumed if a book was banned then it had to be. I went home that day, scraped together my change, and went directly to a shopping center, Northland, I think it was called, where I bought my first book, *The Catcher in the Rye*. I'm not sure what I expected to find between its covers, but I know I read it in bed by flashlight, so I assume I was hoping to find on your pages nude, nubile beauties doing whatever grownups did on their honeymoons. What I found instead was someone much like myself, some-one who didn't fit in, an oddball even among oddballs. It was the first time that I had ever read a book about someone like me, and I went on to read — in short order, actually — everything else of yours that was available in print.

The Glass family became the family I'd never had; interesting and quirky in ways mine was not. What touched me most were those radio broadcasts, or rather who they were for. I mean that fat lady. I'm not sure I know to this day who that woman was supposed to be, or why the performance was to be to her in particular, but I understood the spirit of such advice, and I think it shaped me once I became a teacher. Early in my career I was teaching that passage in an American literature course here at Arizona State. We'd been discussing who we thought she was, why her in particu-lar, why her at all. It's mercilessly hot where I teach, and we begin the school year in the belly of that beast, mid-August. That hot August day in 1977 I left my last class to go home only to find that the battery in my Volkswagen had surrendered to the weather. My car was parked in a heav-ily graveled lot behind the new science building. I went into the building and called AAA, then returned to my car, to my wait. A half hour passed, then an hour as car by car the parking lot emptied, until mine was the only one left. Soon a van pulled into the lot, a new one, a Chevrolet or maybe a Chrysler product, something well beyond a young teacher's budget. It parked adjacent to me, as if starting a row. A lift at its rear lowered, then raised; double doors opened in back. A young man, a boy, really, wheeled himself onto the lift. He balanced his texts on his lap, then lowered himself to the ground. Vans engineered to the needs of the disabled are common now, but this was the first I'd ever seen. With my car on the fritz, I was taken by all those moving parts, by the wonder of hydraulics, by the poetry and magic of a vehicle that works. But once on the gravel, the wheelchair, I saw, was a great disadvantage. Though it was probably less than a hundred feet, I remember it as being a hundred yards or so from the van to the nearest pavement. I recall the sight of the chairbound boy and the shimmer off the rocks in that terrible searing heat. I admired the Herculean effort it was taking to negotiate that distance atop loose rocks toward freewheeling. I offered my help and the young man refused. He'd meant to maintain what dignity he could, but his tone with me was curt, and in return I was rude. I watched in my rearview mirror. It took him ten or fifteen minutes to negotiate that lot, a distance I could have managed in seconds on foot.

I think I understood your writing at that moment more fully than I had ever understood it before, and since that hot August day some twenty-five years ago, I have done my best to teach each class of each course as if I am teaching it for that boy in the wheelchair. I try to teach each student as if they have labored to sit before me, as if anything short of my best would demean the journey that has brought us together.

Jay Boyer

🦋 Jay Boyer teaches at Arizona State University. His plays to be produced off-off-Broadway include *Wollicott's Traveling Rabbit's Foot Minstrels* and *Three Plays and a Bed.*

Dear Mr. Salinger:

If you have the Sunday *New York Times* delivered to your door, you'll
know that on October 6, 1996, the 100th Anniversary Edition of the *Book
Review* reprinted John Updike's critical evaluation of *Franny and Zooey*,
which originally appeared in the September 17, 1961, issue. I did not stumble upon the two youngest members of "The Admirable Glasses" until
some time later, when I plucked the paperback from the racks at the corner newsstand at precisely the time I was experiencing the first throes of
my conversion experience. As you must be aware, conversion is a process
and more than thirty years later, as I continue to tumble about and, occasionally, lose my bearings, Zooey, in particular ("the blue-eyed Jewish-Irish
Mohican scout who died in your arms at the roulette table at Monte
Carlo"), continues to furnish tobacco-free ballast.

I have never had the slightest inclination to read either *The Way of a
Pilgrim* or *The Pilgrim Continues His Way,* but have fretted these many
years over the possible substance of all four (five, really) of Zooey's college
papers on the Crucifixion. For a Jewish girl from Brooklyn who loved Jesus
to distraction but simply could not tolerate the party line, Zooey's take on
Christianity was a teenage iconoclast's dream. Although I exited the local
theater fully convinced, having sat enthralled through *The Greatest* [And
Most Interminable] *Story Ever Told,* it was the Zooey-induced image of
the ascetic Max von Sydow multiplying cheeseburgers and Cokes that
enabled me to *enjoy* the gospel and to explore without self-censorship the
raw material it contains.

But I considered myself a painter then, rather than a writer. I remember
that, at some point during the Summer of Love, I hid a psychedelic depic-
tion of the Crucifixion (stiffly rendered in acrylics and — mercifully — no
longer extant) face down between my bed and the radiator. Were it discovered, I decided, I could point the counter-accusatory finger, for I knew I
would never have been prompted to pick up the blandly packaged *Franny
and Zooey* had not my father, during one weekly outing to the neighbor-

hood library, pushed a battered copy of *The Catcher in the Rye* into my hands with the parental command, "Read this!"

Which brings us to the one and only stumbling block in my acceptance of a more or less generalized apotheosis of the Glass family: Les. Why, Mr. Salinger, is this performer ostensibly at home yet perpetually offstage? Why so clueless in a crisis, so impotent (despite his having begotten seven extraordinary children), so unable to do more for his distraught young daughter than inquire as to whether she might want the mysteriously detestable tangerine? Why do we know so little about Les apart from his former profession? From Zooey, we learn that the father of the Glasses thrives on sentimentality; from Buddy, the narrator (or tour guide) of "Zooey," we learn of Les's contribution to the Glass décor, a manifestation of his pride in his family's accomplishments; from Bessie, that her husband lives entirely (but entirely) in the past, that he has "never faced anything" in all the years she has known him. But we learn nothing from Les himself, because he is not *present*.

At this writing, my own Jewish father is dying of leukemia, having courageously refused a treatment which would in all likelihood have ended his life sooner, and more brutally, than will the disease itself. He is very good at facing things and that is something about him I am going to remember. But I have wondered — even worried, as if they were contemporaries — what the surviving Glass children will remember about Les. I have become suspicious of his very name, as his absence — his invisibility — would seem to imply that he was always of less importance to his children than Bessie, who, in her midnight-blue kimono, looms as large in their lives as Kali, with four whirling arms ever extracting from her pockets cigarettes, matches, toothpaste, pen knives, faucet handles and sometimes, from the steamy atmosphere of the Glass family bathroom, genuine Truth. I've a sneaking suspicion that, had Les wandered into those same vapors on that Monday morning in November of 1955, he would have quite probably disappeared and, what is more, no one would have missed him.

May I tell you a story? I promise you, it's on point. One weekend afternoon, at a mall (of all places), my parents, older brother, and I walked into a restaurant. It was not the type of establishment at which we ordinarily dined, but we had been shopping all morning (for what, in particular, I do not recall) and were too hungry and too weary to care. So we sat at a little round table, and slowly, self-consciously, flattened the intricately folded pink cloth origami napkins, and coughed a good deal, and eventually a waiter in a monkey suit came by with the tasseled menus and, as well, for each of us, a rectangular card on which was scripted, in fine calligraphy, the specials of the day. My father gave this card his close attention, turned it over in his hand, and, after a moment, said, rather wistfully, that he wished he had a stamp so he could mail it back to the kitchen. My mother and brother blinked at each other, but I damn near fell out of my chair. So I ask you, Mr. Salinger, why don't the Glass children have a Jewish father like *that*? I can't help but feel that you have cheated them.

Some years ago a friend who was angry with me sent me a magazine article about you, one which mounted a personal attack not only upon your work but upon your life as you have chosen to live it. This act caught me off guard and, consequently, had the desired effect: I became defensive, not on your behalf but on my own. I apologize now for failing to champion you then, for you have never cheated me. To paraphrase Mr. Updike, your willingness to risk excess on behalf of your obsessions has encouraged me, given me permission, to do the same. My theology, as it developed, at least partially under your influence, now underpins — indeed, almost wholly supports — my own fiction, and for that I am forever in your debt.

> *With gratitude,*
> *Síofra Shaman Skye*

🦋 Síofra Shaman Skye worked as a textile designer in the 1970s, exhibited her paintings in the 1980s, and entered (and exited) a convent in the 1990s. She lives in New York City.

Dear Mr. Salinger,

May I at the outset introduce myself as Dr. Elizabeth N. Kurian who has had the joy and privilege of reading and studying your works. My investigations eventually launched me on a doctoral program that finally resulted in a doctoral thesis on your fiction. I would like to share a few thoughts on a striking aspect of your work, which in my opinion, merits the attention of all of us poised on the threshold of the third millennium.

It appears to me that the plea for silence which is implicit in your fiction and mode of life reflects a contemporary imperative in a world desecrated by the dominion of sound. Silence which is the substance of sanctity emerges as a significant value in your fiction which provides a distinctively religious world-view in an age dominated by secular concerns.

The significance of the dimension of silence is underscored in the lives of all your fictional characters. Holden Caulfield in his disgust and despair arising from his disillusioning experiences conjures up idealistic visions of a life of positive withdrawal in the solitudes of the West. New York epitomizes for Holden the hideous hub of urban life which he finds inimical to the growth of the spirit. He is something like a soul "unknowingly striving to rise from the muck of this world to the peace of Nirvana."

The metaphor of silence is further exemplified in the story of Franny Glass. The Jesus Prayer has thoroughly revolutionized her attitude to life. It is indicated that when the subject repeats the prayer persistently, there comes a moment when the prayer is no longer uttered by the lips; it becomes self-active. Such a meditative practice supposedly enables the individual to gain control over his mind, sense, and the will to enable him to withdraw from the concerns of temporal existence and achieve God-awareness. When Franny awakens to the potentialities of the ethic of silence, she resolves to modify her pattern of life. Accordingly, she hopes to achieve a transcendental experience by nourishing her spirit in the calm of silence and contemplation.

Buddy Glass's secluded life is reminiscent of that of Thoreau who felt that there was constant need for urbanized man to return to nature to realize his higher self. In Buddy's choice of the simple, uncluttered life of the creative writer, it is possible to identify the same abhorrence of the brutalizing forces epitomized in Eliot's "Unreal City" or Fitzgerald's "Valley of Ashes." During a car journey that Buddy undertakes after cancellation of his brother Seymour's wedding, he is instinctively drawn to a fellow passenger — a tiny, silent man. The latter is described as a deaf-mute which should be recognized as a significant symbol in your fiction. Holden Caulfield, as a deaf-mute hopes to lead a life of self-contained existence of illuminating introspection. The concept of deaf-muteness thus becomes a metaphor for silence and reflection which are imperative for the individual to renew himself in the midst of "the madding crowd's ignoble strife." It is possible to observe that there is an increasing rapport between Buddy and the deaf-mute rather than Buddy and his other worldly companions in the car. The episode tries to underscore the tension between the speech and silence that characterizes human situations. An attempt to emphasize the polar opposition between worldliness and holiness and speech and silence is made in unmistakable terms.

The story of Seymour Glass is again a restatement of the theme of silence, a factor of overriding significance in shaping his life and outlook. Seymour exemplifies in unambiguous terms the ideal of contemplation which man has lost sight of in the complexities of a materialistic, fascist culture.

Contemplation is that condition of alert passivity in which the soul lays itself open to the Divine Ground, the immanent and the transcendent Godhead. The story of Teddy also focuses on the significance of the mystical dimensions for an individual's active life on earth. The world of these mystics represents a landscape of silence where they struggle tortuously to a point of self-awareness by imbibing the wisdom enshrined in Zen Koans, the Gita, and the Christian Gospel. Like Thoreau, they immersed themselves in "the waters of silence" and believed that silence and solitude spiritualize the whole man and transform him from a carnal to a spiritual being. The ubiquitous profanation of language and spirit is felt keenly by

Seymour. The distrust of language is implicit in his gesture and statement. Seymour says that "the human voice conspires to desecrate everything on the earth." One of your leading critics is of the view that your object in describing Seymour is to convey in words a life that finds its true consummation beyond words. It is implicit in your fiction that there are actions of the spirit, rooted in silence. Besides, it is also wrong to assume that a verbal matrix is the only one in which the articulations of the human mind are conceivable. The verbal character of western civilization is manifest in the stand adopted by some of its great exponents. The silence of cosmic space, to them, is terrifying. To the Buddhist or the Taoist, that selfsame silence conveys tranquility and the intimation of the supernatural. The highest and the purest reach of the contemplative act is that which has learned to leave language behind it. The ineffable is believed to lie beyond the frontiers of the word. It is only by breaking through the walls of language that the visionary can enter the world of total and immediate understanding. In ultimate truth, past, present, and future are inextricably fused. It is the temporal structure of language that keeps them artificially distinct. The holy man withdraws not only from the temptations of this world, but also withdraws from speech. The Zen Koan "the sound of one hand clapping" is indeed a beginner's exercise in the retreat from the word. In Zen, the verbal correlative to holiness is often a kind of silence.

Silence is not only a significant theme in your fiction but it seems to be also a principle of the form in your later fiction. What you have achieved is to convey the shape and vitality of silence through the unique use of language, as in *Seymour: An Introduction* where the form is shattered and language aspires to a wordy silence. The antiforms of the stories in the form of garrulousness, convolutions, private jokes, sly asides may be apparently repelling but what they demonstrate is that the sacred and the profane are always interfused. That is the reason, vocal as they are, your Glasses also know how to honor silence. It is as if your purpose is to redeem the desecrations of language by parody and discontinuous expression. Artists have attempted the dismemberment of literary forms in an effort to free man from the word habit. The apparent eccentricities that mark your later style can thus be viewed as your reaction against all forms, against language itself. It has been suggested that the verbal flood in *Seymour: An Introduction* is the ultimate exploration of civilized sound which marks an attempt to exhaust that sound and come finally to Zen silence. Your consistent use of the interior monologue is most aptly suited to represent the dialogue the individual carries on with his own inner self in the contemplative phase. It has been noticed that as the focus of the stories moves inward, their outward action declines. The narrative becomes increasingly concerned with internal action. The concept of silence as it operates at the stylistic level serves to strengthen the theme of silence which I have discovered is one of the organizing principles of your fiction. The thematic and stylistic expositions of this metaphor of silence represent a spontaneous expression of the force that chiefly governed the tenor of your life. Your final withdrawal from public life into the wisdom of silence and the privacy of your home is strikingly in line with the distinctly religious nature of your later work and the fictional style whose keynote is conspicuously also silence.

The ethic of silence which characterizes your work is a symbolic expression of man's revolt against the pollution of sound. Your work which can be legitimately viewed as a positive and articulate response to the prevailing temper of narcissism and nihilism is in my view, a major contribution to our age. I'd like to thank you on behalf of several kindred souls for awakening us to an ideal that has long since been forgotten and ignored under the pressure of the new idols of our idolatrous age.

> *Yours sincerely,*
> *Elizabeth N. Kurian*

❧ Elizabeth N. Kurian is a senior associate professor of English at I.I.T. Madras, in Chennai, India, and is a Salinger scholar having done her doctoral work on "The Dialectic of the Active and the Contemplative in the Religious Vision of J. D. Salinger." Dr. Kurian's remarks are based in part on her articles and book about J. D. Salinger's works.

Hiya JD:

A few weeks ago, when the birds were deep into their early morning conversations, the phone rang. Before I could even say hello, a dear friend
tumbled simple words into complex paragraphs that somehow inexpli-
cably entangled with songs of white-eyed mejiros, 'amakihi, and loud
mouthed myna birds. After listening for nearly five minutes, I realized
that she was inviting me to her daughter's wedding scheduled for the first
week in October just when Vermont maple trees would be flashing red
and gold.

Instantly, I knew I wanted to be there and just as quickly I realized that
to travel the six thousand miles over one continent and nearly half of one
ocean was absolutely impossible. More exhausting than the twelve hours
of jet travel were the years that covered that distance with a stubborn
shadow. When I considered those disorganized decades between the last
time I saw Lusanna and this early morning phone call, I knew my exile
was complete and irreversible. The hardwood forests of the Northeast,
once familiar enough to be comforting, had been permanently replaced
by casual, Hawaiian decay of subtropical rainforests, shallowly rooted on
hard skins of lava and centuries of dust.

I first met Lusanna when we were both teenagers prowling about in
NYC's East Village, burrowing through stacks of discarded fur coats piled
on wide-board floors of crumbling loft buildings. Lusanna wanted an ankle
length beaver coat and I was searching for anything that looked appropri-
ately worn and ratty. Lusanna wanted intrigue; I wanted squalor, and when
I told her that, she laughed.

"My mother had this thing about 'squalor,'" Lusanna told me as she
yanked a particularly lush ermine coat from the middle of the stack. The
sleeve ripped free, and she fell backwards, bouncing off a stack of worn
leather bomber jackets. "I always thought her thing with 'squalor' had
something to do with being an English schoolgirl brat at the end of WWII,
but she said it had to do with lace doilies and silver tea-sets. Go figure."

Right then, I knew we had something in common, Lusanna and I. Her
mother was at home in London practicing piano or some such thing when
my father was working for the OSS, drawing political cartoons to be
dropped from planes over Germany. After Lusanna found her coat and
I gave up looking for mine, we drank strong black Russian tea at a little
storefront café on lower Broadway and I amused myself with scenarios of
her mother spying my father in some London pub or at some other awk-
ward social function. In no time, I had them falling in love and marrying,
a neat little trick of the imagination that transformed this beautiful ivory-
skinned girl with pink flushed cheeks from new friend to sister.

Ten years later, long after I had fled to the Pacific and she had settled
down in Vermont to grow flowers, I told her my fantasy, and she reconstructed my fable. We're not just sisters, she said, but twins sharing the
same heart and breathing the same air — even at great distances. We had
been born rather suddenly in the first year of the first decade following the
war when our mother — a wistful yet determined young English girl, only
twenty-two — had found herself in labor weeks before her due date as she
climbed through the rubble of a fishing village where wild rugosa roses
were in ecstatic bloom. She gathered armloads of roses, pausing only
when a contraction overtook her, and then scattered the petals on a small
patch of escaped thyme thick with daisies and dandelions. There she gave
birth to us, two small babies with white-blond hair and red-rimmed eyes.
She wrapped us up in her red-flannel skirts, marched down to the harbor,
flagged a passing sailboat, and sailed back to town, triumphant.

When the town clerk asked for the names of her newborn daughters, she
refused to consider the names of flowers, or even weeds. She was thinking
about chimneys leaning precariously to the left of collapsed garden walls. I
liked Lusanna's version of reconstructed history and adopted it as my own.

My father died in a miserable nursing home in south Florida without ever
meeting Lusanna's mother. In the days before he died, he lay on the high

narrow hospital bed, staring at green-gray walls and a framed print of Van Gogh's sunflowers. By then, speech had left him. He no longer spoke of the secret gun-toting elephants of Europe as he had when the Alzheimer's was just beginning its ruthless siege on his memory.

Two weeks later, at the memorial service, Lusanna's mother put her arms around me and wept silent tears into my hair. Her weeping was so uncontrollable that Lusanna had to help peel her mother's arms from my shoulders and lead her to a comfortable chair by the window. We found her a crewelwork cushion to support her back and packed a number of iced *petit fours* onto a plate. While I entertained the mourners, Lusanna sat with her mother, pouring cup after cup of cambric tea into a bone china cup with roses hand-painted around its rim.

Later, after the last crumb was swept from white linen table cloths, Lusanna took her mother by the hand and leaned against the life-size fiberglass reproduction of Michelangelo's *David,* standing surrounded by faux marble flower vases just feet from the entry door. Lusanna waited until I had shook the last hand and wiped away the last tear before bringing her mother to say goodbye. Her mother shifted her shoulder's back, centered her hat, and reached into her large oversized bag. For a moment, I though she meant to dive face first into the mysterious depths of that great straw bag, but when she reemerged she had a large mailing envelope in one hand and a tissue in the other.

"This," she said, "is for you." She stood still and waited until I opened the envelope.

Inside were three thin paper sheets, yellowed and marked with strange brown patches that looked mysteriously like dried blood. Curious, I pulled them out and laid them on top of the sympathy cards scattered on the low hall table. Turning them over, I discovered that each sheet had a different black and white line drawing printed slightly off-center. One showed a rosy-cheeked woman standing in front of an unfurled American flag. Holding a small baby nestled in one arm, she kept her arm around a man shorter than she with Asian eyes and dark skin. Both were smiling down at the baby and across at each other. In the second drawing, a family sat at a table laden with food. No one at the table looked like any one else and everyone was holding hands. On the wall behind the table, a smiling portrait of George Washington jammed into the crotch of two crossed flagpoles, each pole carrying the old stars and stripes which fell placidly inches from smiling faces of well-fed diners. The third drawing was a careful reproduction of a dollar bill, unadorned. In the lower right-hand corner of each drawing, I could just make out my father's distinctive signature.

"Lusanna's father brought those back with him from battlefields. He told me that some days after a fly-by, those drawings would be blowing about the rubble like so many leaves."

Lusanna's mother buttoned the top button of her cotton raincoat and then unbuttoned it.

"The first time he saw them blowing about, he let them go, but then one caught on his gun and he couldn't shake it loose. So, he looked at it. After that, he started collecting them. He told me once that he guessed a lot of the boys collected them. He found them folded in dead soldiers' pockets and tucked into belt loops. I asked him why he collected them, and he closed his eyes — something he always did when he was disturbed, or worried. He had dozens; I only kept these three. I never knew your father made them."

When I asked her why she kept those drawings and not the others, she pointed first to the aging brown splatters on the still startlingly white paper and then drew her finger lightly over the elegantly curved line of the mother's curved arm.

"They're fragile. The intrusion of blood, this elegant line pulling against the torn paper edge. The humor. The paper. The image. What's there. What's not there." Her voice trailed off, and she dropped her hands. "I love that squalor."

Squalor, for Lusanna's mother, meant that something somewhere had lived, really lived. Squalor marked the heart of beauty. It does for me, too.

Love,
Tia Ballantine

🦋 Tia Ballantine, born in Arequipa, Peru, painted color on canvas for many years in the wilds of Red Hook, Brooklyn. She currently lives with her painter husband on the island of O'ahu where she writes poems and teaches composition.

Dear J. D.,

Let me tell you a teacher's story. It's 1968 . . .

I'm the teacher and Timmy is the student. His eyes smoldered when I told his eighth-grade English class to read a book and write a report. He and I were on opposite sides of adolescence, he a twelve-year-old would-be juvenile delinquent, and I a twenty-year-old would-be school teacher completing a required term of student teaching.

The next day, Timmy showed up not with a book, but with a studied James Dean attitude as he dropped onto a seat in the back row. I called him to the front of the classroom and handed him a copy of *The Catcher in the Rye*. He shuffled back to his desk, sat down, and sighed loudly as he cracked the book.

Timmy's school, an inner-city junior high, was only the beginning of his story. He'd show up with bruises, a swollen cheek, a fat lip. He'd say he'd been jumped by some kid as he walked home from school. The school social worker noted that the bruising coincided with the issuance of report cards and truancy notices, except during a period when his father, a National Guardsman, had been called up for a military deployment. When the social worker and vice-principal visited Timmy's home, they were retold the story of teen bullies who preyed on the younger students. "There's just no discipline anymore," Timmy's father announced. Then: "You've got my permission to do whatever you need to do to beat some sense into Timmy at school. Don't let him get away with anything. And young man," addressing Timmy, "if you come home whining about a licking at school, you'd better be ready for one from me." The vice-principal seemed to consider these words a comfort.

Timmy made no secret of his hatred for school, teachers, parents, or any other authority figure. I had a hard time comprehending how it was that he placed me in that category. I couldn't grow a decent beard. I had reason to hate the authorities, too. There was a war in Vietnam and the draft board was leaning hard.

The bell rang for class change and the students left, except for Timmy. I had to tell him it was time to stop reading and get to his next class. He asked me how they could get away with swearing in a book from the school library.

The following week he turned in his book report, the only assignment he completed for me that semester:

> Timmy
> Book Report
> English
> *The Catcher in the Rye*
>
> This is the first book I ever finished. I thought maybe there were books like this one but didn't think a school would let you read it.
>
> I don't know why Mr. Newmiller had me read this book. Maybe he's just too new. If the principal knew, I'm sure he'd be in trouble. My dad would try to get him fired if he knew about the book. Because if too many kids read about Holden Caulfield, they might start acting like him. Swearing and lying and smoking and getting into trouble and making fun of teachers, and mostly telling things the way they are.
>
> It seems to me that this book shows just how things are. Holden, the boy in the book, is a lot more smart than adults who maybe know more about useless stuff. But Holden knows about what people are really like. He knows that Ackley is a jerk and Mr. Thurmer is phony.
>
> Holden's brother DB is a writer who is a big success in Hollywood, but Holden even calls *him* a prostitute. I think DB is kind of like a prostitute because he is selling. A lot of people in this book are selling, but not Holden.
>
> I'd like to see him when he grows up. To see if he ends up being a father and how he treats kids. I think he will be different from other adults because he isn't afraid to be honest and say what he thinks.
>
> I think what I learned from this book is that there are people out there who can see through crap and write books that are worth the effort. I would recommend this book to all of my friends but I wouldn't mention it to too many adults.

After I finished student teaching, the draft board caught up with me. I joined the Air Force and became a pilot, flying military transports in the Far East — a detour in my life as a teacher. Now, here's a small-world story for you: Once at Yokota Air Base, near Tokyo, I called for maintenance to fix a broken radio on the airplane. I didn't recognize the technician, an Air Force airman, but he recognized me. Ignoring my military rank, he addressed me. "Mr. Newmiller, remember me from eighth-grade English?" I didn't recognize the name on his uniform. Timmy had run away from home when he turned sixteen, and looked back only long enough to change his last name from that of his father to one of his own choosing. He was now Airman First Class Timothy Holden.

The Air Force behind, I've now been a real teacher for a long time. After some thirty years, not much is left to remind me of my student days, but I still have Timmy's book report. On mornings when I wonder why I've stayed in this business that pays so little and demands so much, I take it out and read it. Then I go to work.

Regards,
Bill Newmiller

❧   Bill Newmiller teaches literature and composition in Colorado Springs. He also serves as Editor for Electronic Publishing for the journal *War, Literature & the Arts.*

Mr. Salinger,

It hit me hard when Seymour died. I've had to compose myself in a public restroom. Sending this letter makes me uncomfortable. I don't like to be exposed. But I've been hiding behind the frontlines of cyberspace for several years now, reading letters to you in the middle of the night while I sit in front of the blue glow of my computer. It's disgraceful voyeurism, really. But somehow, I feel like writing this letter today is going to be cathartic so I'm going to go ahead and do it. I finished reading *At Home in the World* by Joyce Maynard several months ago . . . I was sitting in Central Park and my hands were shaking, the light was going down and everything was beautiful and peaceful and quiet. It was disturbing because juxtaposed with the image of the trees and the sky I have this mental picture of you as a frightening old man pointing an accusatory figure at Joyce Maynard in contempt. There was a time when I believed in you like I believed in Seymour. But loving you or feeling contempt for you or reading a memoir of someone's life is all disgraceful voyeurism as well, isn't it? I'm not really sure what I'm trying to get at here. I am miserably uncomfortable when I see someone I haven't seen in a long time in public and usually I try to avoid eye contact. There is something about the polite exchange of public graces that makes me squirm. I wonder why I am writing this. I sort of began with the intention of exposing you, of confronting you, of writing about my triumphant transcendence of the hero-worship that had me hungry to devour every word that you had ever written and make it part of my life. But I am finding that difficult to impossible to achieve now. Because somewhere along the line, some ridiculous part of me that cannot accept that reality as all there is, fell in love with Holden, then Zooey (despite his lengthy, pretentious, largely circular reasoning), then Buddy, then Seymour. And of course, they were all you. The exposed, scared, lonely side of you was Holden, the lost intellectual desperate for answers was Zooey, Buddy was the most honest straightforward you (your alter ego), and Seymour was the you that you wanted to be. So I'm having a hard time listening to the part of me that wants to believe in myself enough to not need to worship heroes anymore. And I think, finally, that that was all I really wanted to say.

Jennifer Flynn

🦋 Jennifer Flynn studies drama at the Atlantic Theater Company at New York University.

Dear Mr. Salinger:

I respect your privacy — never wanted to pry behind your J. D. — never wanted to analyze your novels or be your groupie. Lone wolves commune at a distance, if at all, and though I'm a grownup (supposedly), I advocate parallel play. I'm only writing to you because my analyst insisted — he claims the problem began when my father slammed the bedroom door on my hand when I was four and I missed witnessing my parents having sex. Actually, the signs were there earlier: my mother reports that when I was three, my little brother pointed with glee at a bird whizzing over and my retort was the height of blasé: "Why all the excitement, Danny? You've seen birds before." Had she read the book, she'd have refrained in later years from complaining, "Why, as soon as you get here do you have to go away?" She'd have known then I was destined to be the girl who would be Holden.

When I hit reluctant adolescence, my buddy Bobby, with whom I'd prowled the neighborhood, up to no good, lost his marbles and tried to kiss me. Revolted, betrayed, I bolted away, and later that day I bonked Bobby on the head with a grapefruit heaved from a bedroom window. Before he stopped speaking to me for twenty years, this traitor with the goose egg on his empty head yelled up: "You'll make a lousy girl." This is when I decided that people, including myself, were lousy substitutes for characters in books. I'd trade my beestung, budding breasts, I sighed — I'd trade my sex in a heartbeat — for a chance to be Holden.

The truth is, in high school, with my seeping armpits and bumper crop of zits, I was more like the poor loser — what was his name? — Holden goes to the movies with and ditches. The part of me that would be Holden wished I could ditch myself. Instead, desperate, I went on dates with horny losers who figured a pimply girl would skip the movie and cut straight to the grope. In the backseat of somebody's Buick parked on a dirt road god-knowswhere, as loser number whoknowswhat ripped the zipper on my shorts, I prayed for the power to tell this shallow moron where to go. In fact, if I were Holden, I mused as my glazed eyes watched the dashboard

clock, I wouldn't be prostituting myself for a little affection from the opposite sex. Instead, I'd escape to New York.

Lacking the bus fare, I resigned myself to noble acts — took a cue from my
hero and penned an editorial advocating the transformation of every last
"fuck" to "book." My father, who hadn't read the book, blew his stack and
lectured me from here to yesterday how "no child who slept under his roof
and ate his bread would get away with whorish literary habits like mine."
To avenge myself, I dropped acid and sat at the dinner table gleefully
watching him levitate, float over the pot roast and mashed potatoes, and
burst.

When I finally got to New York I became a traitor myself. What with all
the free-range insanity around me — the duck-woman on Sixth Avenue
quacking at passersby, the dog-man on the subway, the woman on the
elevator scoping out my feet — is it any wonder that now I would be
Seymour? Would want to see less? Would even try to end it all by popping
a bottle of Tylenol and chasing it with sweet vermouth? In the nick of
time, my married lover entered the chapter, drowned me in coffee and
ordered a forced march to the all-night restaurant near Prospect Park,
where I puked on the waiter and the manager yelled, "Junkie get out!"
This was the epiphany that rang down the curtain on divided loyalty —
that finally convinced me I would always be Holden.

Let Bobby and my Dad and my shrink and my ex-husband declare to
their dying day I'm a failure as a girl — I don't care. To tell you the truth
(not that you give a hoot, and that's why I like you), I like being the right-
eously messed-up hero of a book I didn't write — in short, I like being
be-Holden.

Jan Wellington

🦋   Jan Wellington hangs her hat in Mobile where she teaches British
Romanticism and creative writing at the University of South Alabama.

Dear Mr. Salinger:

What an odd thing to be doing — writing a letter to someone who I am fairly certain won't be reading it, and at the same time doing that in a public forum. I guess it's rather like sending off a message in a bottle, except in this case all the bottles are collected and their contents broadcast in something that would be sort of the literary equivalent of a TV talk show. Our voyeuristic audience tunes in on the off chance that one or more of the participants just might say something humiliating or disgusting. Some of us are embarrassed beyond belief — can't believe that we agreed to appear in such a venue. Others can't wait to strip off our tops. Or bottoms. We're all wondering "What will the big guy think?" and "Do you think he'll notice mine?" "Maybe he'll write me back."

I mean, really: It's so un-*you*.

Recently we were planning our literary festival at my university, trying to decide whom to invite and that sort of thing. As always your name lurked just beneath the surface. When you ask students which writer they would like to talk with, the name Salinger always creeps in there eventually. It's often not quite fully spoken aloud, often said with the same resigned longing these young people use when referring to lost high school loves and favorite house pets now gone to their greater glory. Every literate young person in America knows the drill — Get to Salinger: Fat chance. And they never are quite able to articulate what they want from you — I do ask. Over the years I've gotten a pretty good idea. And since here I am with an albeit slim chance of communicating with the man himself, I feel like I should at least float you a message.

The kids all want to say thanks and, also, that they get it. They get what you have to say about being in families and being in school and being fed up and feeling not quite a part of things even though you'd rather like to, if you could just figure out how things worked. They think you are a beautiful writer. They love your work. That's pretty much what they want to say to you.

And, what do I know? You very well may decide to spend some afternoon browsing your way through these letters. Maybe there are old friends represented in the collection, or former friends or colleagues. Maybe someone against whom you've harbored a longstanding grudge. Certainly you are curious. So you are browsing and come across my letter, a writer you more than likely have never heard of. And then, what? What goes through your head? Are you bemused? Contemptuous? Do you say, "Hey, I really appreciate the fact that Dave passed along what the kids are thinking." (Who am I kidding? The kids send their own letters all the time. Do you get those? What do you think of those?) Actually, I think I have a pretty good idea — even though having an idea like that is, again, so un-*you* — this whole thing is so ironic!

Anyway, as the kids say in their letters, thanks for reading and thanks again for the great books. Write back if you get a chance.

    Your devoted reader,
    David Haynes

P.S. To anyone reading this whose name is not Mr. Salinger: You are reading SOMEONE ELSE'S MAIL. What's up with that?

❦   David Haynes is the author of seven novels for adults and five books for children, including *Live at Five* and *Somebody Else's Mama*. He teaches at Southern Methodist University and Warren Wilson College.

Dear J. D. Salinger,

Your book, *The Catcher in the Rye*, has become a sort-of second Bible in my life. I am a senior in high school, and I first read the book when my cousin, David, recommended it to me the summer before my freshman year. Growing up, I had plenty of friends, yet I felt desperately lonely at times. It wasn't that I wanted to be popular. I just suffered from manic depression and low self esteem. I nearly never speak in class, except when I feel passionate about something. My peers are always encouraging me to speak up more often, and that they are highly interested in what I have to say, but, again, I have low self esteem.

I spent much of my teenage years searching for answers, inspiration, and security. I found all this from Jack Kerouac (*Dharma Bums*), Russell Banks (*Rule of the Bone*), jazz, blues, punk rock, acid rock (Pink Floyd), and so much more. I also spent a lot of time going to punk shows. For six to eight dollars, I could see four bands. Not only that, but the band members would walk around and talk with the fans after their band had played. It was so unreal to shake hands and converse with people I highly respected. These weren't the rock star sellouts that I deeply hated and, to me, a hand-shake and a few minutes to talk was worth more than a superficial auto-graph could ever be. I respect punk rock because they were so intensely against major labels, selling out, and MTV. It felt good to know that my six to eight dollars was going to support an underground scene that was strug-gling to maintain noncorporate standards.

Now here comes the part where you might call me a sellout and/or a hyp-ocrite. I plan on going to film school to write screenplays for movies. I know what you're thinking, that I'm going "to Hollywood to become a prostitute," but I'm really not like that (at least I seriously pray that I'm not). I am inspired by movies such as *Clerks, Chasing Amy, Dead Man Walking, Stand By Me, Trainspotting, Destiny Turns on the Radio, Pump Up the Volume, The Breakfast Club, Platoon,* and so much more. I guess what I'm trying to say is I like movies that have something to say and I believe a good movie has a plot that revolves around more than just millions of dollars in special effects.

Anyway, I loved your short story, "A Perfect Day for Bananafish." Your technique in this story continues to amaze me. I may be wrong, but it seems like you tried to make the whole story slightly dull and slow (much like real life is like), only to shock the reader with the suicide at the end. To me, this is saying that even seemingly well-adjusted people can be seriously depressed and/or suicidal. This story moves me, because a friend of mine committed suicide after killing his girlfriend. He was the last person in the world I would have suspected of suicide let alone murder. Another story I loved was *Franny and Zooey*. I can relate, because, my two sisters and I often break into arguments when trying to have civil/peaceful conversations. Sibling relations are better these days, and *Franny and Zooey* will always be a part of my heart and soul.

I won't wish you "good luck," but I do hope you find that peace of mind that we are all searching for.

Gene Woo

❧ Gene Woo was born in Seoul, South Korea. He is a junior at the University of California at Irvine majoring in philosophy.

Dear J. D. Salinger,

Twice in my life I've encountered your work: first with nervous perplexity at age nineteen, then at age fifty-five with surprised excitement — and a sudden desire to draw your epiphanic "portrait." I'll explain.

Catcher didn't help me grow up; instead, it mirrored my adolescent frustration in the summer of '62 as I immersed myself in a four-hours-daily course at Indiana University, preparatory to a study tour in the Soviet Union. Though the Carnegie Foundation (scared by Sputnik, like many of us) was paying most of my way as a guinea pig in their language learning travel experiment, I didn't know why I was studying Russian, beyond the pleasure I felt in the language itself — gorgeous wild sounds and intricate grammar. I had hoped for insight into "big questions" from those "universal" writers Tolstoy and Dostoyevsky but found I couldn't relate to Levin mowing hay with peasants, or strange nightmares about inquisitors. My bad conscience about living simply for the present, in the day-to-day enjoyment of exotic language games only became worse when I sensed Holden's own plan-less, moment-to-moment moods. He seemed oddly arrogant about his private randomness, not bothered in the least, while I feared becoming what my parents called a "drifter," a "hippie," and all. When Russians in a Moscow park asked me if I had read *Nad Propast'iu vo Rzhi* (Over the Abyss in the Rye) I said yes, but could add little more. Franny and Zooey and Buddy and Seymour couldn't help me either, as it proved: from their lives I took away only an impression of vague religious syncretism and deep discontent.

But at fifty-five, when I had given up fruitless metaphysical questions for answerable aesthetic ones, studying now the irreplaceable individual epiphany patterns of our major modern literary "seers" since Wordsworth, I was ready to read all your books again. On finishing them I knew that you were one of the truly valuable epiphany makers in the Proust-Joyce tradition, and in an article for *Style* (34: 117–31) I attempted a detailed portrait of your epiphanic sensibility. Here's a quick summary sketch; I would be fascinated to know (if you'll pardon the chutzpah) what you think of it, since you're the only living author who has ever "sat" for one of my pictures.

Your epiphanies are about art (heightened and refined sensation, artistically conveyed in precise, painterly dabs and spheres or circular forms), childhood (its remembered happiness and simplicity embodied in bright, pure colors), and the pleasure and pain of nostalgia for childhood's loss and possible sudden recovery (evoked in hide-and-seek or *fort-da* scenarios of disappearance and return). The girl whom Zooey sees, with her tam the red color of Van Gogh's blanket, pops out from behind a tree to rejoice the heart of her frustratingly leashed, green-collared dog. When Holden, whose own red hat has just been comfortingly placed on his head by Phoebe, sees his blue-coated sister making her reassuring reappearances on the circular carousel, he weeps with unexplainable sad happiness. Making one more (semi-)circular (re)turn, Seymour's imagined little girl sweetly turns her doll's head to look at him, in a haiku written shortly before his suicide. Pain and joy fuse as another of Seymour's haiku personae is bitten by a resentful white cat while he gazes at the round white moon. Sometimes a return may be only longed for: Franny would like to fall asleep in a poker chip of sunshine on a café table, or to sink to the watery depth where in spidery light she can recapture a can of bright gold medal coffee. Or a melancholy absence may yet figure a return of bright, childlike, airy life, as in another of Seymour's haikus when a disconsolate woman finds a spring-green toy balloon on a bedspread, in an apartment not far from Central Park. Even when loss is final, there would be — for Buddy — a comfort for a dying man at the foot of a hill if only he could accompany, with his eyes, the graceful form of a woman bearing a perfectly balanced jug over the hill's rounded crest.

Bright colors, rounded shapes, aesthetic intensities and precisions, hide and seek, childhood's loss and possible recapture, hopefulness and pain, sad triumphs. These, to me, are your treasures; this, your epiphanic portrait.

With gratitude,
Martin Bidney

🦋 Martin Bidney is a professor of English and comparative literature at the State University of New York at Binghamton, and is the author of *Patterns of Epiphany: From Wordsworth to Tolstoy, Pater, and Barrett Browning.*

Dear J. D. Salinger,

How is it that so many people know your novel, but routinely get it wrong? My guess is that not many of them have actually read it. Such is the fate of literature, I suppose, especially the few books like yours that become part of our heritage, or go "hyper canonical," as Jonathan Arac puts it. Holden, for one, is not a rebel, as many seem to think. He's sexy, but no sex maniac. Above all, he's not a psychopath. It must be maddening for you to hear Holden likened to assassins and serial killers. (Stand down, Mark David Chapman wannabes. No one cares what you read.) And it's too easy to see Holden as a case of arrested development, traumatized by Allie's death, unable to mourn. That interpretation is at least grounded in the text, but isn't that the kind of psychobabble that Holden himself doubts?

It's hard not to think of your book largely in terms of Holden, and I'm just as guilty as is everyone else on this count. Holden's a helluva guy. He really is. He's kind, careful, insecure, and lonely. He hates change, loves children, worries about the ducks. The graffiti at Phoebe's school infuriates him. FUCK YOU gets him steaming. SHUT UP is unbearably obscene. He's obsessed with preservation, with mummies and museums, Eskimos forever frozen. Idolizing Jane, he never calls her. I love that. Holden wants to do the right thing. Maybe he's hypocritical, immature. He tells us that outright. Maybe he's even a tad phony. For a guy who hates the movies, he's sure seen a lot of them (he's taken Phoebe to see *The 39 Steps* ten times). He might not even be the catcher in the rye. I'm guessing that could be Phoebe, who saves the broken record pieces, saves Holden, really. Holden knows it. It's very ironical. Did you hint at that?

I know people wonder about your literary influences, and it's hard not to play that game. Holden might be more at home in a New York taxicab than aboard a raft, but he's not so different from Mark Twain's Huck Finn. Holden's also optimistic and clever, if a bit clueless. He, too, is the American boy, for better and for worse. His story is also called countercultural, but it's part of our repertoire. There's more to Holden than Huck, of course, and here I'm talking about the bard, speaking of Literature proper. Hamlet's in the mix, as your earliest reviewers were quick to note. Holden, after all, is haunted by a ghost, partial to monologue. (Still, some were dissatisfied; *The Christian Science Monitor* compared you to Shakespeare and found you wanting.) You haven't given us much to go on, but I'm sure you had other role models for Holden. Maybe Roquentin in Sartre's *Nausea* (1938), who wanders the streets of Paris in an existential funk? Holden, too, roams the metropolis, cataloguing every encounter, every detail. He too confronts the Nothingness of Self. Or am I just reading too much into it?

By the way, I'm one of those flits—"damn perverts"—that Holden worries about. I wince a little when I read such lines, but still I'm impressed by the boy's relative maturity about queer people. Or yours, so soon before McCarthy and so long before Stonewall. Holden seems almost drawn to flits and lesbians, or to places where they hang out. He's a little freaked out, too. Homosexual panic almost seems a rite of passage for adolescent boys, although that's slowly changing. But to call Holden homophobic doesn't explain much. When his teacher Mr. Antolini pats Holden's head in the middle of night, Holden panics and bolts, but he remembers how nice Mr. Antolini has been, even worries about his reaction. "I wondered if maybe he just liked to pat guys on the head when they're asleep. I mean, how could you tell about that stuff for sure? You can't." One of the teachers' guides I looked at—a pretty new one, posted on the Internet—completely revised this section in a chapter summary: "Holden spends the night on the couch at Mr. Antolini's house because he is so gracious to Holden." Can you believe it? But no one wants to admit the homo-dynamics of *A Separate Peace*, either.

I teach adolescent or young adult (YA) literature at the college level, and what really interests me is how *The Catcher in the Rye* helped pave the way for other stories of bright, introspective, and vaguely alienated boys. Every spunky kid in fiction is the newest Holden Caulfield—or so publishers hope. Thanks to you, YA writers know how to fuse the search for identity with irony, cynicism, and a mild despair. There's a bit of Holden in every self-conscious Paul Zindel narrator, in every disaffected, eccentric teen character. Condescension and self-loathing mix and mingle in today's adolescent angst.

There's also the narrative framework that you pioneered. Holden tells his story in retrospect, living in "this crumby place," some kind of treatment facility in California. And at the end, he talks about a psychoanalyst who asks dumb questions about Holden's future. So the whole book is a story that Holden shares with the reader, as he's thinking about his life and at least pretending to get better. We see this framework again in S. E. Hinton's *The Outsiders* (1967), seen as the first official YA novel. Ponyboy Curtis also tells his story after the fact, trying to heal wounds and to survive Johnny's death. And to meet an English assignment (this was the origin of *The Outsiders*, written by the sixteen-year-old Hinton for a class) Ponyboy knows that "Nothing Gold Can Stay"—but Johnny's dying words are "Stay gold, Ponyboy. Stay gold . . ." Ponyboy gets a new start. Holden may, too, but he's not so sure, and neither are we. Telling Holden to "stay gold" would be like writing in his yearbook, "You're a helluva guy. Don't ever change." He reminds us that storytelling has its price, that writing and healing aren't necessarily wedded. "Don't ever tell anybody anything," he says at the end. "If you do, you start missing everybody."

Maybe the best example of this kind of set-up comes from Robert Cormier's *I Am the Cheese* (1977), about a boy whose life is disrupted by political violence and an early version of the Witness Protection Program (being developed even as Cormier worked on the book). Cormier uses three levels of narrative, and we never know which one is most current. In one, Adam rides his bike toward Vermont in search of his father; in another, he is interrogated by a "doctor" who turns out to be an enemy (the third is Adam's memory). Through the sessions, Adam remembers he is really Paul Delmonte, and reconstructs the devastating chain of events that destroyed his family. The novel ends with him in a mental institution, riding his bike in circles within its gates. Cormier fuses *The Wizard of Oz* with *The Catcher in the Rye* to produce a harrowing book.

Adolescent fiction seems welded now to the idea of the psychological, so I guess it's not surprising that so many YA novels portray their heroes as slightly maladjusted, and do so in an "intimate" format reminiscent of your novel. The latest spin is Stephen Chbosky's *The Perks of Being a Wallflower* (1999). Charlie is a more sedate version of Holden, who tells his story through an even more classic epistolary format. He's writing to a mysterious stranger, mailing each chapter as a letter. And he, like Adam-Paul, suffers a serious breakdown, finally remembering an episode of sexual abuse, in keeping with our contemporary spin on dysfunction. Here's how the novel ends: "So if this ends up being my last letter, please believe that things are good with me, and even when they're not, they will be soon enough. And I will believe the same about you." Not so melancholy an ending as Holden's, but similar enough in readerly address.

And then there are the little details that reverberate. I'll end with just one — Allie's baseball mitt, a leftie with poems written all over the pockets and fingers. The mitt explains Allie, and helps us understand Holden. Holden wants to be the catcher, after all. Turns out, baseball mitts and baseball are everywhere in YA literature, though that's hardly your fault alone. Sometimes it's good and sometimes it's wretched. In Chris Crutcher's *Staying Fat for Sarah Byrnes* (1993), for instance, Ms. Lemry waxes nostalgic about the baseball mitt she was forced to relinquish to boy players. Sounds okay and even usefully feminist when I summarize it, but she's way out of character. It's an embarrassing moment in an otherwise compelling book.

Victor Martinez turns the mitt to better advantage in his beautiful *Parrot in the Oven: Ma Vida* (1996) winner of the National Book Award for Young People's Fiction. Here's a book dramatically different from yours, but weirdly in the tradition you helped establish. Set near the Mexican border in the Central Valley of California, the book begins with Manny Hernandez and his older brother Nardo picking chili peppers in the summer heat. Manny wants money to buy a mitt. Exhausted, he daydreams about baseball, about a different sort of field: clean, green, and cool. Watching an older man picking fast and furious, he sees "a terrific shortstop." Then suddenly immigration officials sweep through, dividing the pickers into teams, the legals and the illegals. Manny still thinks baseball: "We all cheered and waved our arms as if our side had won." He longs to play. As the first chapter ends, Manny dreams about the mitt, "all clean and stiff and leather smelling," and wonders how long he'll have to work to buy it. "The weariness of it," writes Martinez, "stretched as wide as the horizon." So much for the field of dreams. So much for the fantasy of play, and of rescue as well. Manny and Holden are on their own in the existential sense, even if Holden has material resources far beyond those of a barrio boy.

The Catcher in the Rye is not entirely unlike Holden: funny, complex, stuck in time and space and yet weirdly alive. That's why I like it. Thanks for writing it, and rest assured that I won't expect you to write back. No *Finding Forrester* fantasies here. No kidding.

> *Respectfully,*
> *Kenneth Kidd*

Kenneth Kidd is an assistant professor of English at the University of Florida. He is working on a book project called "Boyology and the Feral Tale."

Dear Mr. Salinger,

Thank you for the pleasure of reading *The Catcher in the Rye*, and for its timely words. I am a sophomore in high school and have found your sincere images to be so very, very relevant to the life that I wake up to and expect daily. In your chapters I beheld the ordinary travail of teenhood carried above the ordinary sense of life in a writing you stitched so shrewdly together with the character, Holden Caulfield.

I noticed that many of Holden's triumphs were deep, internal triumphs, and that the beauty of his adventure is a deep and internal beauty. From a lifestyle saturated with TV and adolescent peers, I gather that the world often looks past inner glory and inner beauty. Superficially, Holden's triumphs appear painfully few, as a microscopic ecosystem appears from a macroscopic point of view. However, from a point of view nurtured with *The Catcher in the Rye*, I am eager to believe that the world is twice removed from correctness — once for triumph and once for beauty.

I read *The Catcher in the Rye* for an English class this year. We were assigned a paper to write on the book, and I was sorely disappointed that many of my friends skimmed over the book purely for the purposes of the paper. I chose (with encouragement from my teacher) to put aside time to explore what I could of the novel's bottomless depths — a glad toil that has, to my dismay and delight, taken several readings and many days (I am a slow reader). However, I have found that the time I set aside to walk through *The Catcher in the Rye* instead of running through it has paid me back a hundred times, not only by giving me even a vague understanding of what I never understood before, but also by allowing me a fresh wonder at the potency of literature.

I cannot help but bring out at this point one of my mother's reminders at the Food Land the other day. She reminded me, while we were fingering through the oranges in the produce aisle, that the brown-speckled, pitted, and undeniably ugly oranges were the sweetest oranges.

Coincidentally, after my friends' cursory leafing through *The Catcher in the Rye*, I have noticed, after regular inquiry, that many of them have in addition never tasted the sweeter flesh of an ugly, prosaic orange. Most buy wallpaper yellow, glossy as the day they fell from the tree oranges from the Food Land (never ugly oranges), just as they never selected *The Catcher in the Rye* for a diligent reading. For those that have (concerning oranges in addition to *The Catcher in the Rye*), I hope they have been rewarded as I have been, with an internal and secret kind of sweetness that deepens their love for books, their appetite for oranges, and indeed, their appreciation for adolescent life.

I am too embarrassed to recount for you the individual passages that intrigued me (believe me, you and I would be here for a long time), but I will only say that I was most profoundly touched by those images closest to what I observe every day. Holden's interaction with public transit, the schools, the streets, and the people in between, for example, all rekindled some memory of yesterday, or last week. The other way around also. Here in Hawaii there are many ducks and ponds, and ducks swimming in ponds (although the ponds don't freeze like in *The Catcher in the Rye*). It was only a few days ago that I was driving past a duck pond on the way to school thinking about Holden.

I think the attention and hidden glory given to the otherwise pedant images in *The Catcher in the Rye* trickles asunder from the pages of the novel into the otherwise pedant images of my life. The novel reminds me to give attention to the duck pond on the way to school, to wonder about the people I meet in school and on buses, and to "glory" in likewise familiar scenes. When maturity and adolescence are weighed, pound for pound, passage for day, I would say that the daily images of my life contributed to my appreciation for *The Catcher in the Rye*, and that likewise the novel contributed to a new appreciation for my life. I would like to thank you for both, and everything in between, because I fear that there is much left for me to thank you for that escapes my head at the moment, and this letter if you ever get a chance to read it. But, that is of little importance to me because I know you will receive many letters from important and adroit authors who can thank you more effectively, and in greater quantity, than I. That was the original intent, after all, and these paragraphs present my personal attempt.

Sincerely yours, with your novel in mind,
Michael Mashiba

❧ Michael Mashiba is a junior in high school. He plays the violin and piano and participates in baseball and golf. This is his first published work.

Dear J. D. Salinger,

A quick note of thanks for helping to make my Hero & Antihero in American Literature class successful last fall. You see, we had been viewing and talking about James Dean in *Rebel without a Cause* and then moved immediately to *The Catcher in the Rye*. And my students picked up on Holden and ran with him and Jim Stark (the James Dean character) for two weeks.

Let me tell you a little about my students. I work for a university with a student body that is 67 percent Latino and whose family incomes qualify most of them for food stamps and federal financial aid for college tuition. Half of my students have to have part-time jobs, sometimes more than one, to make it through college. They are fairly bright, not exceptional, but are socially and politically involved with their city. The city, San Antonio, Texas, reflects the makeup of our student body. It's 56 percent Latino, predominantly Hispanic, but is closer to 66 percent Latino when we look at just the college age population. That percentage was reflected in my class. All of the rest were Anglo.

You might wonder what a fairly unwealthy group of students might see in Holden Caulfield and Jim Stark that would appeal to them. Frankly, so did I. We talked about that a lot. They began by thinking Holden was fairly "phony" himself. Rich kid with an attitude, a sense of irony that they had developed themselves over years of living in substandard housing in fairly bad areas of the city. "What the hell has he got to complain about?" they asked. And Jim Stark prompted the same questions. "Look at them both: well off, good opportunities for education, able to spend money on cabs, trains, and cars. Wish I had what they have!"

But, as they reread *The Catcher in the Rye* and saw the film again, their attitudes began to change. Not all of them, but a good number of them. At first, they had somewhat grudgingly enjoyed your book and the film while not being able to identify very well with either Holden Caulfield or Jim

Stark. As they thought more and more about both, they began to identify, if not with the circumstances, with the attitudes of the two characters. They thought Jim was cool, but a bit too much of a good guy. They couldn't sympathize very much with his reaction to being called "chicken," but did identify with his standing up for his rights and for Plato's rights. They loved Holden's wit, his basic outlook about the phoniness in the world. Eventually, they started quoting some of Holden's best lines. There weren't very many great lines worth quoting in *Rebel without a Cause*.

So, Mr. Salinger, this letter is to let you know how a group of fairly poor Latinos and Anglos came to appreciate your book. I don't think any of them will ever forget Holden Caulfield and *The Catcher in the Rye*.

> *Thanks much for writing it.*
> *H. Palmer Hall*

❧ H. Palmer Hall is the library director and teaches at St. Mary's University in San Antonio, Texas. His fourth book is *Deep Thicket and Still Waters*. He is also the publisher of Pecan Grove Press.

Dear J. D. Salinger,

I remember when I cracked open *The Catcher in the Rye* in study hall at Longfellow School for Boys, the English master, Mister Didsbury, was impressed. "You're much too young for that book," he said. This was 1959. I was thirteen, a year older than most of my classmates though there were some even older. Longfellow was where they sent all the malcontents and/or stupid boys who couldn't make it in the other schools in the Washington, D.C., area. My parents sent me the year before from public school when I flunked sixth grade. I think that in 1959 I was like Holden Caulfield after the novel was over or at least that's what I believe, that he returned from that "crumby place" in California to find, like myself, a school where the adults were, if not always trustworthy at least harmless, and the students were good co-conspirators.

I loved *The Catcher in the Rye* enough to remember after all these years that Holden hated phonies and loved his sister Phoebe because she was so innocent. I remember him standing on a hill overlooking the football game after he was kicked out of Pencey Prep. I remember he went to New York and that there were a lot of elevators in the novel. I forgot Maurice. Recently I reread *Catcher* and I felt like Holden when he went into the Museum of Natural History and saw all the exhibits frozen in time, the Eskimo that "would still be just finished catching those two fish, the birds [that] would still be on their way south." Yet he was not *frozen* which is the way I feel after all these years, to see Holden *still* standing on the hill overlooking the game after forty-two years while I have changed in a thousand different ways and so has the world. And this is what both bothers me and makes me feel good, at the same time.

Mr. Salinger, I think, when you wrote this book, in a sense, you opened Pandora's box. With all those "goddams" and "Chrissakes," and the sarcasm and anger at all things inauthentic, you let out into the world a revolutionary idea. Adults are not perfect. The rules they make up are not perfect. The world sometimes *stinks*. This was true, if I remember correctly, back in those days in my area of the country. The Potomac River was a cesspool. The sky was gray and overcast every day. Blacks were segregated. Wars were all over the place and we didn't feel bad about getting into another one. And the bomb hung over all of us. So no wonder you hated the phonies.

What bothers me after all these years is that we have swung the pendulum in the opposite direction. The Potomac River is clean enough to swim in. The sky is blue most days unless it's about to rain. The bomb may not be as much of a threat. And I am a member of AARP and maybe that's the problem, that I am a card-carrying adult, worse, a senior citizen. So much has changed and so much has stayed the same. I think you opened Pandora's box, you and Froggy the Gremlin, the Beatles — it was no surprise to me that Chapman was carrying your book when he shot John Lennon. You and Timothy Leary, Martin Luther King, and all the rest helped to create a world hardly recognizable, a world not as comfy as the one I grew up in when Mommy used to stay home. A world full of disaffected youth and I include adults in that category. Bart Simpson. Eminem. Liberal Democrats. Conservative Republicans. Even Ren and Stimpy. I hear the voice of Holden Caulfield all around me now. If imitation is the sincerest form of flattery, I think you've been flattered to death. I only wish that you were around today with an older and wiser Holden, the one at the end of the book who, if not exactly a member of the Optimist Club, comes to realize that he misses "everybody I told about. Even old Stradlater and Ackley, for instance." This is the Holden I like the best, the one who sees the humanity even in the phonies and, I think, must come to see some *phoniness* even in himself. It is one thing to be disaffected. It is another thing to make a career of it, as in the case of Chapman, Bart, and even some liberal Democrats. That is a dead end street.

With Affection,
Jeff Richards

🦋 Jeff Richards's essays and fiction have appeared in many newspapers and journals including the *Houston Chronicle, Gargoyle,* and *Radio Void.* He lives in Takoma Park, Maryland.

Dear Mr. Salinger,

During the past three years, we have used your novel, *The Catcher in the Rye*, as the focus for an online discussion between two very different sets of students: a high school class in a suburb of Chicago and a college class in rural Kentucky. The Web forum is held each September, when the high school students are beginning their senior year at Benet Academy and the college students are in the last stage of their training as secondary English teachers at Murray State University. When we first thought of bringing our classes together in an electronic discussion, we weren't convinced the project would work since the two groups seemed worlds apart. What is clear now, however, is that Holden Caulfield can unite students of varied ages, interests, and economic resources, if not in agreement, certainly in relevant and sometimes heated debate.

Although we provide the prompts for some of the discussion threads and require our students to complete a set number of postings, we usually step back from the exchange, allowing the students to assume control of the conversation. They soon become intensely engaged in the online chat, posing questions, offering interpretations, and even sharing links to relevant Web sites. Invariably, the threads that provoke the most varied and emotional responses are those dealing with Holden as a character and those addressing the value of teaching the book in the secondary classroom.

Even though you created Holden more than fifty years ago, the students today still see a part of themselves in him. One of the high school students, Dave, explained, "Holden is easy to identify with for all teenagers, for he is struggling to come into his own, face the world, and decide if he agrees with everything that is going on in it." Another senior, after admitting, "I am very Holdenish," invited others to explain how they saw themselves mirrored in this protagonist. The response to this prompt was phenomenal! Students spoke of being "not yet an adult and no longer a child," of longing for the simplicity of their younger years, of hating the game-playing they associate with growing up, and of wanting to protect even younger children from the ugliness of the world.

Through your book, students are moved to question themselves. Kelly attested to this fact when she wrote, "Holden made me look at things differently. He made me look at my own life to see if I was playing the game. I didn't want to be a phony." Holden intrigues these young people. The complexity of his character calls forth fairly sophisticated analyses — from diagnoses of attention deficit disorder and chronic fatigue to claims that he is "a self-contradicting, irony-laden hypocrite." Jeff saw him as "both honest and a liar, both mature and immature, both loving and misanthropic," and Wesley labeled him a "human oxymoron." Diana provided even more insight: "There are two dueling parts of Holden's character — one that would like nothing better than to completely change the world but also another part that wishes he could escape from society completely. He's running, not only from all the 'phoniness' in the world, but also from himself."

Thank you, Mr. Salinger, for creating a book that engages adolescents, that prompts them to critique the world around them, and that continues to haunt all of us who have read it. One of the best testaments to the lasting power of your novel came from Shannon, who confessed, "I finished the book more than a week ago, but it is still with me. For example, in the grocery store the other day I wondered what Holden would think of all the brainwashing we receive by packaging and brand names in the store. . . . J. D. Salinger's writing style has also stuck with me throughout the week. I find myself saying certain *Catcher* phrases such as 'it killed me' in conversation and writing."

Those training to be teachers benefit greatly from being exposed to Holden and from seeing the way high school students react to him. Soon, they will be teaching young people who will undoubtedly exhibit the same angst and the same mixture of cynicism and idealism that we see in Holden. To become the kind of teacher that Mr. Antolini represents, they must recognize the complex emotional lives of adolescents. The Web forum is also useful in preparing these future teachers for the level of sophistication that they can expect from classes on the secondary level. The Benet seniors, who are enrolled in Advanced Placement English, are bright and engaging, eager to challenge interpretations made by their fellow students and their teachers. With any luck, by being exposed to the articulate and insightful comments of adolescents early in their training, the college students will be less likely to deserve the censure Holden delivers: "You don't have to think too hard when you talk to a teacher."

Although the postings from the Benet students should make it obvious that your book is an excellent choice for the high school curriculum, the college students from rural Kentucky, who tend to be from very conservative backgrounds, usually have misgivings about teaching controversial works. When these future teachers voice their concerns online, the high school students become quite vocal in arguing against censorship. We want to share a few of their eloquent responses with you:

Mac: "Saying that *The Catcher in the Rye* is not for adolescents is going against the whole purpose and message of the book. Ignoring the swearing and the sexual content, which is as much a part of adolescence as school and drivers' education, the book centers on the struggle of Holden, a teenager, to fit into and make sense of the adult world. How much more appropriate of a topic can there be for high school students?"

Suji: "I'm sorry, but if you think that teenagers don't drink, smoke, or have sex, then you are living in an alternate reality and you need this book to bring you back. On another level, however, *Catcher* is hardly going to influence teenagers to go out and have sex. I disagree with the idea that the reader necessarily sees Holden as a role model. I see him as a character that I can relate to, nothing more, nothing less. If I can pick out a character in a novel from an AP English class and empathize with his situation, then I wholeheartedly believe that the text is appropriate for school."

Steve: "My Dad loved *The Catcher in the Rye*; who would've thought that more than three decades later, it'd be just as important and relevant to me as it was to him. *The Catcher in the Rye* is banned for the lifestyle it portrays by people who perfectly fit Holden's description of 'phonies'; they are ignorant, judgmental people who ignore the underlying message and ban things for superficial detail. As long as conservative adults do that, kids will read the book; as long as there are kids like Holden who are atypical outcasts and get pushed around by peers who mindlessly play 'the game,' this book will be near and dear to teenagers."

Besides prompting these wonderful defenses, the discussion about whether or not *Catcher* is appropriate as a school text also leads to worthwhile analysis of language, heroes, and the purpose of literature. What more could we as English teachers ask of an online discussion?

If you ever want to see a sample of the conversations your novel still has the power to elicit, please feel free to visit our Web forum at this URL: <http://campus.murraystate.edu/academic/faculty/carol.osborne/forums/eng529/threads.cfm>.

Each September, two new sets of students will be logging on to give their impressions of Holden's "whole crummy story."

Sincerely,
Carol Osborne and Mike Stracco

Carol Osborne directs the Humanities Program and teaches contemporary literature and English education at Murray State University. Mike Stracco has been teaching high school for twenty-five years in Illinois. He also teaches an integration of writing and photography at the College of DuPage. He has four children ages ten to eighteen.

Dear J. D. Salinger:

Virginia Woolf claimed that writing fiction was all about developing character but really, she was in love with sentences, with language and her
ability to shape it. You, on the other hand, knew how to develop character
through voice. It's a voice that cannot be duplicated on film. It has that in
common with Woolf's fiction and with most of the best fiction. It is interior. Your characters live and breath but mostly they think and talk. They
argue with themselves and with others. The action is minimal. The drama
is internal. There is a thin line between sanity and craziness. They may
crack at any minute. Yet they are witty and urbane. They are well-read.
They smoke cigarettes and pace and lie down on couches and drape themselves over chairs. They take long baths. They lose things. They tend to
exaggerate and criticize one another. They are really funny and sometimes
foolish. You have that Chekhovian ability to create characters who are
endearing and a little bit foolish but never fools.

They may describe themselves as freaks and outsiders but we identify with
them against the world. More so when we're young perhaps. This is, after
all, the quintessential American adolescent position. And as children and
teenagers we are not yet corrupted or at least we don't yet see ourselves as
being so. It is everyone else, adults in particular, whose motives are suspect. It is the other people in the world who are phonies and liars and who
are pathetic. Like your principle characters, we see ourselves as complex
and we struggle to puzzle life out.

As adults, we leave it to our artists to retain these traits and they pay the
price for taking such a stance. They alone must be true to their vision,
must sacrifice themselves for their art even if it means drinking themselves
to death or blowing their heads off. Yet all of us, like your characters, harbor dreams and want to see ourselves as doing what we can.

You are an urban writer. The exterior world, the setting, does not seem to
be particularly important in your work. There are few descriptions of the
outdoors. Even with interiors, you describe the contents of a room quickly

to advance the sense of character. A scene might take place in the bathroom or the living room or the dorm room. Plot, for you, is not exactly action-oriented. The tension lies within and between your characters.

Mr. Gregory, my eighth grade English teacher, called *The Catcher in the Rye* the boys' bible, but it wasn't just for boys. Holden's whine in 1951 developed into a cultural movement in the sixties. Like Holden, we believed that the only way to deal with rampant conformity was to rebel against it. But we weren't checking into the hospital for a rest. We weren't being psychoanalyzed. We were marching in the streets, growing long hair, dressing the way we wanted — calling into question the values of a country that appeared to have grown too complacent. It didn't seem like enough, the American dream of living in a house in a suburb and believing in America right or wrong. Love it or leave it didn't give us enough room to move. Holden Caulfield was right.

Most adults then and now perform roles in order to achieve an agenda. Even if it means the Orwellian staging of international incidents in order to start a war. As always, in the sixties, those in charge had no idea how steeped in illusions they were. They didn't even seem to know they were phonies. They didn't know that the world was more complex than they saw it, that Vietnam was a quagmire, literally and ideologically. Holden knew what was wrong but he wasn't sure what to do about it.

Revolution, tear down the walls, "open the doors" as Whitman said, that was our mantra. Ultimately, like Holden, we weren't sure what it was we wanted. Well, we wanted the war in Vietnam over and the troops home, a less materialistic society, an end to racism and sexism. We wanted to dismantle the class structure. But then what?

We found ourselves in Franny's shoes. She was a woman on the verge of a nervous breakdown. We brought the entire country to the verge of a nervous breakdown. *Franny and Zooey* was published in 1961 — ten years after *The Catcher in the Rye*. You were way ahead of the curve. You anticipated the longing for spiritual fulfillment, the turn to eastern religions and the universality of religious beliefs. Franny repeats the Jesus Prayer: "Lord Jesus Christ, have mercy on me," but she is not doing her rosary. She is repeating a mantra, engaging in mysticism as a way to stay afloat in a world full of fakes like her boyfriend, Lane, and her English professor, Tupper. Her brother, Zooey, trumps her by insisting she has to live her life and develop her talent because she needs to act for the fat lady in the audience — the fat lady who is Jesus and Jesus, Zooey tells her, is in all of us.

From our perspective it is now easy to see the postmodern elements in your work. The way you seem to move into and out of fiction and nonfic-tion: "what I'm about to offer isn't really a short story at all but a sort of prose home movie. . . . The fact is, I've been producing prose home movies, off and on, since I was fifteen." What we now call the authorial voice seems to be heavily invested in Holden in *Catcher* and in Zooey in *Franny and Zooey*. When Zooey rescues Franny from her nervous col-lapse, he does so by feeding her spiritual nourishment from the *Baghavad Gita*, Epictetus, Tolstoy, and Kafka. A formidable group to attempt to refute even now. When Zooey has finished with his message, Franny has recovered and is blissfully content.

Today we're a little less likely to take this as the straight self-help program that critics saw it as in 1961. We'd still like to believe that spirituality will get us through, that if we are true to the Supreme Being (a nice politically correct term) we will be happy. None of us really wants to admit he is obsessed with the fruits of his labor. We want to believe that it is always about the work, the work we were meant to do. In *Franny and Zooey* we hear this message coming to us not from some guru (nearly all of them have been discredited), and not from those vaunted experts of the popular magazines, with their Ph.D.'s in psychology, and not from those founts of wisdom who write the lyrics of pop music and rap, but from a recluse, a hermit, a guy who wrote one novel and a number of short stories. We can only conclude that such a fellow might like to believe what Zooey believed . . . on good days.

J. D. Salinger, your fiction remains subversive. Holden, like Huck, takes a stand against society and pays for it. Franny is as naïve as Billy Budd and she walks the plank. Yet Franny and Holden and Zooey and most of the Glass family endure the crucible. One commits suicide. The rest are stricken like Job yet they take their stand and invite us to join them. They may get a little preachy or cute or sentimental but they don't give in and get civilized and they are not condemned to death or hanged as witches. They mostly survive, if barely, on shaky ground. Just like the rest of us.

So that's about it, buddy. Not that you really want to hear about it. Not that you're listening. Now that I've written it, I'm sort of sorry I wrote it. I guess I sort of miss you. That's the problem with writing about someone. You end up missing him.

Sincerely,
Ed Meek

❦   Ed Meek has published articles, poetry, and fiction in the *North American Review*, *Paris Review*, *Boston Globe*, and *Yankee*.

Dear Mr. Salinger:

I entered your world in college when I read "For Esmé — with Love and Squalor" because of the title. It drove me slightly title-mad even as an academic writer, throttled me higher when I later turned to creative writing. Your early work introduced me to Oriental unhappenings née happenings. I have written what I call "green rice shoot" poems and stories.

As a college president, I gave a talk on "Whatever Happened to Holden Caulfield?" The title was merely a springboard into the horrors (not to say "phoniness") of the old chestnuts and platitudes, but one pre-/post-reaction stays with me. After the announcement in the campus paper, an Asian student made an appointment to tell me how "delighted" he was with the topic. "Mr. J. D. Salinger was one of the first to appreciate Oriental minds." I was unable to convince this young man that the forthcoming address would not illuminate him further about the "mysteries of Mr. Salinger and Mr. Caulfield." When I proceeded out of the auditorium that day, he was waiting. He looked at me and just shook his head, though gently, to be sure. I knew failure as I had known the fatuity of stereotypes from the moment he appeared in my office; you turned that inscrutable Asian "scrutable."

When I saw the call for these letters, I bought a copy of *The Catcher in the Rye* to reread on my way to Valdez, Alaska, with a play (*Resurrecting Trolls*) competing in the Ninth Annual Last Frontier/Edward Albee Theatre Conference. John Guare was this year's honored playwright, and I finished *Catcher* just prior to attending an evening showing of the film version of Guare's *Six Degrees of Separation*. I was not familiar with the play or the movie and was stunned to hear the "dazzlespeak" of the young Black con artist about Holden and *Catcher*. My latest play, *Rain Games*, reacts to that experience and to *Catcher*. Below is an excerpt.

Jo-Jo is a fifteen-year-old girl passing as a boy because of a terrible act her mother has committed against her. Nonnie Nellie is a rich widow masquerading as a bag lady. I am shocked to recognize that, as Guare's Paul points out, Holden "folds at the end" when it starts to rain. *Catcher* has perhaps influenced *Rain Games* far more than I yet know.

Jo-Jo. (Nods.) When you were my age, you went whole-hog about everything. Age has tamed you.

NONNIE NELLIE. (Laughs.) Not quite. When I was your age . . . well, let's just say I was *semi*-free, not *hippie*-free, even then.

Jo-Jo. And your husband was less free and made you even less free.

NONNIE NELLIE. (Laughs.) God no! He was a college professor. That's as close as you can get to free without being a hippie in some people's book. Hey, Kid, did anybody ever tell you —

Jo-Jo. — that I ask weird questions? Yes, all the time.

NONNIE NELLIE. Well, I for one like them. They remind me of Holden Caulfield asking cab drivers and assorted other so-called adults where the ducks of Central Park go in the winter time when the lagoon freezes over.

Jo-Jo. Why's it called a "lagoon"? If it's in Central Park in New York City, why's it called a lagoon?

NONNIE NELLIE. (Laughs.) I never thought of that.

Jo-Jo. Have you seen *The Sopranos*?

NONNIE NELLIE. Only one episode. Last Christmas. My son and daughter were home. They were scandalized by the "concept," though they hadn't watched it. I had to see one. I loved it. Next time I'm home, I'll watch it. Why?

Jo-Jo. Tony Soprano worries about the ducks flying away from his pool.

NONNIE NELLIE. No sh — kidding?

Jo-Jo. Do you think Holden Caulfield grew up to be Tony Soprano?

NONNIE NELLIE. (Laughs, then goes serious.) You've read *The*

Catcher in the Rye, then? I wasn't sure. You know about all the criminal types who spout it, love it?

JO-JO. Criminal types? No. Mel Gibson was always buying a copy in that conspiracy movie. He played the good guy.

NONNIE NELLIE. You and I must take a trip to the local library. Don't worry, I'm known, respected there, have a card. I want you to read a play by John Guare. *Six Degrees of Separation*. You haven't by any chance read it, have you?

(Jo-Jo shakes his head no.)

NONNIE NELLIE. Thank God, or I really would think you were playing the prodigy game with me. It's bad enough that I already think you're one of my six degrees. A *high* one of my six.

JO-JO. What?

NONNIE NELLIE. You'll have to read the play for that, too. But mainly for the Salinger. This young Black guy — about as pretty as you and gay, incidentally — scams these high-muck-a-mucks in New York. That he's been shot by a mugger. That he's the son of Sidney Poitier and knows their children.

JO-JO. It doesn't sound like an adult made it up. How old is this dude who wrote it?

NONNIE NELLIE. It doesn't, does it? (Makes a check in the air.) Mark up one for our side. Mr. Guare is older than I am. That's G-u-a-r-e. Anyhow, in one of the Black kid's speeches rigged for dazzle, he talks about *Catcher* and all the real criminals who've adored Holden. It's a *tour de force à la tour de bullshit*. One of many. Which would make them *tours de force à la tours de bullshit* just in case you want to quote me or appropriate the material as your own. I wouldn't want to think I've spawned any *tour de forces*.

JO-JO. (Making the Boy Scout pledge sign.) Scout's honor and hope-to-die, I will speak it correctly *and* cite the source.

NONNIE NELLIE. Good, rare boy. This is the fiftieth anniversary of *The Catcher in the Rye*. I think Mr. Salinger would like to meet you. If you pull it off, ask him one for me. He's "caught" everybody with Holden. Everybody but a few crabby critics who think he's had it too easy. But nobody has posed the real question.

JO-JO. Which is?

NONNIE NELLIE. What's the *rye?* Not "where's the beef?" What's the *rye?* You can't be a catcher without the rye. What is it?

JO-JO. Most people can't be catchers *with* it.

NONNIE NELLIE. Out of the mouths of babes and sucklings. (Shrugs.) I'll put away the rye for the next rain time. It'll be my next rain game.

So, Mr. Salinger, with all respect, I ask, "When will we have the novel about Holden grown up?" He could use your help.

Thank you.

Sincerely yours,
Lynn Veach Sadler

🦋 Lynn Veach Sadler is a former college president in Vermont and a full-time creative writer.

Dearest J. D.,

You don't know me, but what I hope to show you is that, really, you do.
Just as I have come to know you without knowing you. I am writing this
letter like one does a message in a bottle. I have an intended audience —
you — yet I know the chances of you reading this are slim. It's different
from a letter one writes and sends in the mail. It's different from today's
electronic correspondence. And it is so very, very different from what one
might say in a phone conversation. I think perhaps . . . yes, I think it is
more like a private journal entry. You are my subject and you are my
addressee.

I had a professor once who studied and loved your work like none other.
No one left his class not knowing your name, not knowing at least one of
your stories. Seymour was real to him. You did that, J. D., you made characters live lives beyond your pages. He even named his dog Holden. And
as I sat in my first class with this professor, you became a mist in my imagination. It had been awhile since I had read *The Catcher in the Rye*, in high
school I believe. And I hadn't heard your name since. Yet there you were,
a faint image I somehow longed to bring into focus. But you don't allow
many to do that — do you, J. D.?

And as I went from class to class with this professor, as I transformed into
what he deemed a writer in my own right, it was as though you too were
a parent figure. You were always coming in and out of our conversations.
When we talked of the struggle of making characters real — we summoned
Seymour and Holden. When I became defiant and believed writing was
an illusion, that it was making my life worse by the minute — we summoned the stories of your seemingly reclusive nature. Why would Salinger
remain so distant? If you wrote a book that has spent so many years on
the active lists of libraries, if you reached people in such a profound way,
wouldn't you want to take ownership? Wouldn't you want to make sure
that what they thought they believed about the story was what you
intended?

I have had some struggle in my life, J. D. I have lost a family and fought to rebuild it again. I have fought to teach myself how to live with one foot in everyday life and the other in the realm of Lorca's *duende*. I'm a college lecturer myself now, teaching my first Intro. to Lit. class, as a matter of fact. And do you know what? Not a day goes by when I don't stand in front of the class and realize that professor of mine is with me, and so likewise, you too are with me. Somewhere along the line, you came into focus. The more I've struggled, the more distinct you have become. The writer's life. It's something that can't be taught, can it? We can tell our classes about the life of Hemingway or Whitman — or Salinger — but we can't tell them about what it feels like to lie in bed at night feeling guilty, not because we've done some horrible deed, but because we've not done justice to our characters in progress. And there really isn't any way to explain how this life puts you in ironic opposition to life itself. Thomas Mann knew that. Spent his entire life trying to draw some kind of an alliance between the two. If I could, I would hold you and tell you, "Though I don't know you, perhaps in some small way — I know."

May the *duende* continue to make you scream out into the dark night for all the days of your life.

> *Sincerely,*
> *Jenn Gutiérrez*

❧ Jenn Gutiérrez teaches English composition at the University of Southern Colorado. Her poetry has appeared in the *Writer's Journal* and *Texas Review*.

Dear J. D. Salinger,

I introduced John Updike to an audience at Franklin and Marshall College, where I teach, by pointing out that we had many things in common. For example, we have both been writing for the pages of the *New Yorker* magazine since the late 1950s. I let a long pause develop, so that the audience could take in the full import of what I'd just announced — and then I added that among the things that John Updike and I don't have in common is that the *New Yorker* printed his words. I feel much the same way about writing to you. I've been writing about your work for more years than I care to say, and if I had to choose between a dream in which you scrutinize each of my sentences and (luck of luck) like one or two of them, or the grittier reality which tells me that you don't give a fig about what an English professor says or teaches about your work, I guess I'd choose the latter.

What I have to say here is simple enough: Thanks. I realize that you've had more than a few hard knocks thrown your way in recent times, and that fame and privacy simply don't go together in our tell-all, sensationalistic society. You need another intrusion, even by letter, like you need another request for an interview. But since I've already said what I wanted to say, I'll let your characters continue to speak for themselves. However, should you care to write me back, that would, as they say, make a slightly aging English prof. very glad.

Sanford Pinsker

🦋 Sanford Pinsker is Shadek Professor of Humanities at Franklin and Marshall College. He is the author of *The Catcher in the Rye: Innocence under Pressure*.

Dear J. D. Salinger,

Of course you remember how you get Muriel to paint her nails in "A Perfect Day for Bananafish" in preparation for one of your least assuming, and, in a poet's opinion, one of your greatest sentences: "She was a girl who for a ringing phone dropped exactly nothing."

Perhaps it will amuse you to know that I have referred many aspiring poets to that syntax. Poets, obsessed with the line, forget the rhythmic possibilities of a simple sentence that doubles back into the sequence of ordinary word order. How grateful I am that you did not write, "She was a girl who dropped exactly nothing for a ringing phone."

Sincerely,
Molly Peacock

Molly Peacock is the author of five volumes of poetry, including *Cornucopia: New and Selected Poems*. She is poet-in-residence at the Cathedral of St. John the Divine and the online poetry consultant for the University of Toronto School of Continuing Studies.

Dear Mr. Salinger,

Talking through a phone line with no person at the other end is a strange thing. You hear the bell-like static. You realize it is the blood rushing through the canals of your own ears. The phone begins to beep and then you put it down and talk to yourself without the formality of the receiver.

I've done a lot of study of your work. And what I've realized is that by studying you, we are studying that person on the other end of the line. By removing yourself from the equation, you make us realize that ultimately the illusion of a voice is really the echo of our own words, even words that we haven't said yet.

You're a strange cipher, Mr. Salinger. I don't know what to make of you. I love your writing and part of it is what inspired me to be a writer myself. But it puzzles me, this phone business. Because you'll never read this. You'll never read one of my stories or even hear about my appreciation of the way you've made my experiences just a little more special, just a little more tinged with beauty and sorrow.

I don't know when the last time you read your own books was. Maybe you read them all the time, maybe they no longer exist for you — thirty years old as they are — but do you remember the Davega bicycle from *Seymour: An Introduction*? I'm sure you do. You're staring at your pale cream, slightly fingerprint stained telephone, nodding absently, flicking your eyes to a bookcase and then back again. I always saw the Davega bicycle as the supreme gift that required involvement in the complex and dull ritual of reciprocation but just engendered in the giver a feeling of even and perfect happiness like the steady buzz of a telephone before the number is dialed. Thank you for your Davega bicycle, I ride it daily and always make sure it is well oiled.

Thank you for the mysteries, the Gentleman of Shalott I have in my head. Thanks for nothing, thanks for everything.

Camille Scaysbrook

🦋   Camille Scaysbrook is a novelist, playwright, screenwriter, and director from Sydney, Australia.

Dear Mr. Salinger:

I want to take this opportunity to thank you not only for the enjoyment
and insight that your work has given me and my students for many years
but also for the profound change that your work has brought about in my
life.

Back in the 1970s, when I began to teach your fiction in college courses,
I came across the dissertation of an Indian graduate student by the name
of Sumitra Paniker who reported that you studied at the Ramakrishna-
Vivekananda Center in New York. She also mentioned that you gave a
copy of *Franny and Zooey* to the Center's director, Swami Nikhilananda,
with an inscription in which you say that you wrote *Franny and Zooey*
"to circulate the ideas of Vedanta."

In order to understand the role that Vedanta plays in your fiction, I bought
all the books I could find on the subject and took a six-month program of
courses at the Ramakrishna-Vivekananda Center under Nikhilananda's
successor, Swami Adiswarananda. I also attended the Center's summer
retreat in the Thousand Islands which — so I was told — you had attended
in previous years.

After immersing myself in the Upanishads, the *Bhagavad Gita,* and the
writings of Shankaracharya, Ramakrishna, and Vivekananda, I became a
convert to the *karma yoga* ideal that Buddy and Zooey Glass advocate in
Zooey and *Seymour: An Introduction.* As a result, my purpose in life
changed from solipsistic self-realization to doing my daily duty with all my
might without hankering after the fruits of my actions. To this day, I shine
my shoes for the Fat Lady even when I am not going to be in front of an
audience.

Wishing that you may write many more works and change the lives of many more people, I remain in gratitude,

Eberhard Alsen

🦋   Eberhard Alsen has published several books and many scholarly articles on American literature. Two of his books are on romantic tendencies in twentieth century American fiction and two are on J. D. Salinger.

Fools flatter. To the wise, flattery is meaningless, insignificant. The wise remain aloof, away in some far off place. A wise man will not be caught glorifying himself in the blind gullibility of society. The wisest of men have never been heard, for they have never spoken to the grand audience of fools. The fools would only praise and worship them, not listen. They would dissect, probe, analyze, scrutinize, consider, question, and investigate everything the wise man had taught them, not listen. The wise man creates art, he works wonderful magic and delves into forbidden and long lost ideas, and he tells no one. Society hunts the wise men. It stalks them. When they are found so is their brilliance unearthed. Exposed, the brilliance crumbles under society's obsessions. The wise are to be left to think, discover, and create. The fools are to ignore, and live their fruitless, pitiful lives in darkness.

Dustin Sebell

🦋 Dustin Sebell lives in Wayland, Massachusetts, and attends Wayland High School. His favorite authors include Joseph Heller and Dalton Trumbo.

Dear Ex-Neighbor,

That's the term that will best describe our tenuous relationship by the time you read this letter (if you bother to). We've now both been living in this town for more than eight years, but to my knowledge I've never set eyes on you. You're not a very community-involved person. If you were interested in helping the local library or historical society keep going, we certainly would have met, for I have been active in both of them, and I wonder who will replace me if my departure is even noticed.

Just as when I came to town I made clear that you had nothing to do with it, so my going hence has not been influenced by you, either. I've liked Cornish very much, and I can see why it appeals to you; but it's time for me to be moving on. The main reason for my selling out in Cornish is that while it continues to provide just the retreat *you* want, for me it has proved a gradually disillusioning experience with the minuses now outweighing the plusses. I came here because I wanted to get to know the region where my ancestors had lived for several generations, and I carry away many treasured memories; but now, like them, I'm moving on — the roving kind. I guess with the passing of my mother, who found Cornish such a pleasant retreat two years ago, along with a failure to keep the house restoration going along as well as I would like, the town has now become too haunted for me; and after eight memorable summers and some other good times here, I hope to be off to Europe. You won't be hearing from me again anyway unless Twayne Publishers decides I should revisit your writings, twenty-five years after my first report on them. "Good riddance," you'd probably say if the event were brought to your notice. I wish it could be, "Wish you luck and long life." Anyway that's my final turnoff to you. I'm surely glad that a naval colleague told me I should drop Herman Wouk's *The Caine Mutiny* when it was a bestseller in 1952 and read *The Catcher in the Rye*. I did — not just then, but many times since. I like your writing. I have a feeling that despite no comment you have read at least something of mine, and I feel sure that the feeling is not reciprocal.

Fare thee well,
Warren French

PART THREE

From the Web

"All of a sudden—for no good reason, really, except that I was sort of in the mood for horsing around—I felt like jumping off the washbowl and getting old Stradlater in a half nelson."

—J. D. Salinger, *The Catcher in the Rye*

Dear J. D. Salinger,

It has been ten years since I've read a short story of your's, by accident, in an old issue of The Saturday Evening Post. From there on it was a hunt to find everything you've had in print. At first I wanted to thank you for all the great characters and stories you have given to your readers over the years. I mailed 2 letters to your home in NH and I am sure you either threw them away or told the postal workers to treat it as an "Occupant" letter and had them discard it in the most effective of ways — an incinerator.

I decided to become a writer myself after reading all your books believing that I could change the world with stories, and unlike yourself, Mr. Salinger, the people who wanted to discuss my stories with me have been welcomed to questioning what why and how I did what I did. I can't say I even like you as an artist anymore, Mr. Salinger, because no artist who wanted to disappear would continue to have his books published. He wouldn't make an issue of not being an issue and most importantly, he'd get over what was bothering him after a couple of years. So, 30 years later you keep yourself hidden in your house, with your fence and mystique and people continue to read Catcher. Your vanity keeps them from reading great stories like, "The Inverted Forest," "The Long debut of Lois Tagget," and "Soft-Boiled Sergeant." I'll have to credit you for giving me the drive to write Mr. Salinger, but like a child who hates his father, I will never forgive you for playing the pretentious artist. You didn't want to be treated like God, yet you act one by "existing", knowing that we all believe you're here but can never talk to you or see you. We can read your books but never really know now if you believe a word you've written down.

I am sure this isn't the first time you have been criticized for acting like a debutante with far too many things on her mind. I just can not explain how angry you make me. I don't think I have even put one cohesive sentence together here because the whole concept of this page has me overly excited that if you read this, you might smarten up and rejoin the human race.

At this point all I can do to explain my rage is say that you and Raymond Carver are the best short story writers who have ever lived and it is a shame that Ray passed away and you are still with us but refuse to be alive. Thank you, mr. Salinger for disappointing another person you inspired. I hope you burn everything you have ever written before you die because I really can't take anymore of you at this point. Good luck, Mr. Salinger.

Jimmy J. Pack Jr.

I hope you never read this.
I do not find you dear.
Simply the embodiment of an eternity.
Without which there would be less purity, hope, decency in the world.
And you believe in none of these.
Niether do I.
Don't be obscene.
Try to listen for once.
This was your disease:
You never learned to receive.
But I have a taste for vomiters,
For hunger in an abyss,
I have a sharp desire to violate you
Because your nudity is not nudity
It is art, and yet honesty.
A gift:
I ate each page.

A. B., 17

Dear J. D. Salinger:

I think what you have done to American teenagers is a disgrace. Holden is
a whining spoiled brat and does not represent the majority. I think Catcher
In the Rye has every right to be banned. You have created a cult of slackers
whose idol you are. They are throwing away their lives just to be like your
lousy fictional character, who also threw away his life. I attend a private
high school in Chicago on a scholarship and my family lives on public
assistance. I recieved a partial scholarship to Princeton University next
year, and I have no idea how I'll get the rest of the money. I think of people like Holden, who have loads of money to spend on fancy Ivy League
schools and instead flunk out, and it makes me want to spit! I'm sorry, Mr.
Salinger, but I don't agree with your message. I do, however, think you are
a good writer. Too bad you wasted your gift on dreck like "Catcher In the
Rye." I'm sorry to just slam everything you ever put on paper, but I'm also
no fan of the Glass family. It would be nice if you could expand your hori-
zons and stop writing about the upper class. I live in a lower class black
neighborhood, I'm not ashamed to say it, in what is called the "ghetto"
part of Chicago. My apartment building is peopled with drug users and
alcoholics, but there are also people who are intelligent and witty, but
have lost all hope. Some of these people are more interesting than your
characters, and you should write about these types of people and thus
appeal to a broader audience. Good luck in all of your future endeavors,
however. Thank you for listening.

Jamal Carter

❦

Dear J. D. Salinger,

******This is not a letter to J. D. Salinger*******
The idea of a book of letters written to J. D. Salinger really sucks. I've
often thought of writing a letter to Salinger, as I'm sure you and others

have or have done. But, J. D. Salinger doesn't need any letters from any of us. As you said, the book will be an open forum for us (the admirers of J. D. Salinger) not for or to J. D. Salinger himself. I think to attempt to write or visit J. D. Salinger betrays what Salinger has stood for, for the past 50 years. He's not a sell-out. His silence supercedes anything you can put into print and by striving to publish you miss what would truly be a book to and for J. D.Salinger — no book at all . . .

David Miller

❧

Dear J. D. Salinger,

I have just finished reading some of the other letters which might be included in the "Letters" book, and I am beginning to understand your reasons for being such a recluse. God! These people! Why do people feel it necessary to explain what was already explained in your writings. You think that they believe that they were the only one's who cracked the code . . . if there even is one? Whenever people say "It changed my life" don't you just want to vomit? Shouldn't other things be changing these peoples lives, and aren't things changing their lives everyday? I mean like when a movie is sold out or when you forget your glasses when you go out to eat and the person sitting next to you says "you always forget your glasses when we go out to eat, don't you know to bring them by now?" People just seem to like to ruin things, but the funny thing is that sometimes we want them to be ruined in a unknowing sort of way. It's like when your about to see a movie, sorry about over using the movie analogy I know YOU use it often, and before you go see the movie you read someones own take on the picture in the newspaper. Nevermind that this person is getting paid to write the review, and that you don't know him. We just feel it necessary to take a strangers advice, and more importantly his interpretation on the film until the point where we come out of the movie either agreeing with the critics points or disagreeing with the critics points. Why can't we just let things stand alone and come out without anyone's knowledge, and when somebody does read or watch something which has just came out, then nobody else can read or watch it anymore, only new things can come out for the person who could not read or watch what they did not read or watch. Anyway, thanks.

　　Steven Hopkins

🦋

Dear J. D. Salinger,

Would you agree that you really know no more than the next pathetic schmuck and that like a lot of men you drink too much and ravish younger women?

🦋

Mr. Salinger,

I always get a headache after finishing one of your books. It takes me weeks to reflect and absorb. I ate up everything. I actually live in a place where everyone's a complete phony, except for my dad. My head aches all the time. You helped me do what I really want to do and become what I really want to be.

I'm 16.

　　thanks.
　　ida

Dear J. D. Salinger,

this is such a coincidence because I've been meaning to write you a letter and there I was surfing the internet and found this page. Well, dear J. D. Salinger, how are you? I hear you're pretty old now, like 80 or something, and I'm 19, struggling and desperate to be a writer. Guess what? I just read "young folks," and it's so the essence of your style, just not as a developed as in your later works. I was in search of this piece like it was the meaning of life because I wanted to see how I compared to you when I reach 21. Actually I wanted to see if I was better.

Right now I'm in writing class and workshops and lit classes, and I don't know why we don't study you. Your work does what I think fiction was meant to do, inspire. For a while I was wrestling with what was better, The Illiad, or Catcher. That poem inspires, Achilles is fucking the MAN, but Catcher does too, on a more modern level. It's also written with such sympathy — for holden, phoebe, phonies, me, my parents, the author.

I just wanted to say that I want to write like you, and that to me, you're that writer that every aspiring writer has to look to for beauty.

> *Thanks,*
> *Albert Pulido*

❧

Dear J. D. Salinger,

The Catcher in the Rye was one wierd book. I read it this year in my English class. I am still very confused about the meaning of the story. I don't understand what is going on inside Holden's head. I personally think that it was a waste of time and money writing this book. Now, I know that this book is very famous and it means a lot to every one but, what is it all about. The least you could have done was made an ending that made sense. It ended so abruptly that I found myself staring at the last word

disapointed. I want to read the book over again to try to find some meaning to it but, I don't think so. I hope to read more of your books later on in
the future. You should keep writing because you seem like a very good
writer that just had an off year while you wrote that book.

Sincerely,
Matt Hatfield

❦

Dear J. D. Salinger,

I'm Holden, who do you think you are writing about me? Leave me and
my life alone.

Holden

❦

Dear J. D. Salinger,

When I was younger, a friend of mine bought me a hardback copy of
Catcher in the Rye for a graduation present. In the jacket, he wrote me a
touching note regarding our friendship and the changes that our lives
would presumably take after graduation. In the note, he misquoted David
Bowie. My friend wrote, "David Bowie once said, 'Time may change me,
but you can't change time.'" What Bowie actually sang was, "Time may
change me, but you can't trace time." Obviously, his misunderstanding of
the lyric parallels Holden's erroneous belief that the Robert Burns poem
actually said, "Catch a body coming through the rye." I never said anything to my friend about his mistake. I just let it go.

E. Graf

Dear J. D. Salinger,

Hey I think that you are a confused person. The way you talk about how
everyone is a phoney bastered and has no clue about the world. I think
you are the one who does not have a clue. Who in there saine mind would
go off into the woods and live by themself. What went so wrong in your
live to become so closed off to the world. I don't understand what you talk
about sometimes in the book. You are very intresting but you are some
what crazy. But that is ok. Well I hope you work things out in your own
little world and enjoy being by yourself and alone.

   Bouc

   ❦

Hey JD,

i was wondering what you were doing tonight. maybe we could hook it up.
im awful thirsty.

   little jimmy

   ❦

I can't say that I liked your book but I can't say that I hated it either. I can't
relate to Holden's negativity and hatred towards the world, but I can relate
to his hatred towards the fake and phony people in it. What I don't understand is why he feels this way about them since he is the one thing he
hates the most. Although he wants to see himself as the "catcher in the
rye", why would he be trying to save the children from the very thing he
has failed in saving himself from? I have known many people so far in my
life and most of them are as phony as they come, but as I continue to meet
people, I am continually amazed at how realistic some of these people are.
These are the people I try to surround myself with in order to get a true

perspective about what people truly think about their surroundings as they move into the adult world. I don't think that Holden ever took the time to really get to know a person in order to understand who they are because he is so quick to label them as phonies. Maybe he would have realized that all people aren't phonies and that there actually are a lot of people who view the world in the same way he does. But because he put labels on people before he gets to truly know who they are he sees everyone as materialistic and fake. I have found that people only become phonies in order to impress you, but if you open up and get to know the person that they really are, you get a chance to see the real world in the eyes of someone else. I think that if Holden would have done this he would still see the adult world full of phonies but also full of many people who don't follow the so called fads and who live their own lives the way they want to and not how society says that they should.

Tulula Bohm

Dear J. D. Salinger,

I wrote a song that sums up my feeling on "The Catcher In the Rye". It's sung to the tune of "Oops! I did it again" by Britney Spears, in case you've ever heard it:

Oops! I read it again!
This real crappy book!
I'll give it the hook!
Oh Holden, Holden!
You are a whining shrew!
I'm so glad I'm throughhhhhh . . . . .
Reading this piece of trash!
Oh, Holden's problem's are not real
They're just all in his head

I really wish that he were dead!
I cry ever-y day
When I see this book
I keep it at bay
But to lose this novel, that'd be just fine with me!
Oh, Holden, Holden!
(Repeat chorus)
Anyway, the book stank, in case you didn't figure it out. Sorry.

🦋

Dear J. D. Salinger,

In English we recently had to chose a quote that best sums up an author's life/philosophy. In my opinion that is a stupid assignment, but since you are one of my favorite authors I chose you. How do you think this quote sums up your philosophy?: "With music strong I come / with my cornets and my drums / I play marches not for accepted victors only / I play marches for conquer'd and slain persons." (From "Song of Myself" by Walt Whitman). I love your works and thank you for listening!!

Lianne

🦋

Dear J. D. Salinger,

ppppppppppppppppppphhhhhhhhhhhhhhhhhhhhhffffffffffffffffffffffffffftttttttttttt
ttttttt

Dear J. D. Salinger,

You know what, Mr. Salinger? Thanks for nothing. You just go about your little, tepid business of writing and burning and leave the rest of us to live this life. You just want to be that character in your stories, that tough guy like Seymour Glass who's really nothing inside. You're the Chief, leading the adoring Comanches around and baiting us with hollow stories like the "Laughing Man," all the while chasing something better, some Mary that won't love you. You don't recognize that all the world waits breathlessly for some sign of you, yet you do recognize it all the same. What you have done with your life now is a tragedy, and I wish that I had never read any of your work, because I know it is only emptiness, it is a void that I so desperately pine to fill. Your work is nothing to me. It is so beautiful that I hate it, because I can only know one thing that follows each page I read. It is nothing.

> *Sincerely,*
> *Adam Klinker*

❦

Mr. Salinger,

As much trouble as Holden had growing up, gaining acceptance, and finding his direction in life, it is my belief that acceptance was never what he was looking for. No, Holden was way too stubborn to relate to others, they were all a bunch of phonies, right? You never wanted to gain acceptance from your book. You didn't want so many people relating to your book. If so many could relate, why wasn't Holden accepted? "Isn't it ironic, don't you think." My question to you is, how do you feel knowing there are two million Holdens running around out there . . . ? I'm sure this, your book never intended to accomplish.

> *Adam DeHaven*

Dear J. D. Salinger,

My upstairs bathtub seems to be draining poorly. I was wondering if you have any ideas on how to get it unclogged. Thanks in advance.

Kernsy S. Byron

P.S. We know you have been peeking at these letters.

❦

Oh J. D. Salinger,

Every time I'm in a cab that smells all vomity I think of you and Holden and say so, usually to the cab driver, and all of a sudden it's a perfect day, really, for more than bananafish, more than anything at all.

polly

❦

Dear J. D. Salinger,

I bet sometimes you wish you were a deaf mime too, just as sometimes I do. Ah well back to staring out of the window!

Yours
Pete :)

❦

Dear J. D. Salinger,

Question: Can time really stand still?

peter hall

Dear J. D. Salinger,

I have just recently finished reading "Shoeless Joe" by W. P. Kinsella for the second time in 5 years. I was surprised to see the author that Kinsella characterizes is not Terrence Mann (as in the movie "Field of Dreams"), but the author of my favorite novel, The Catcher in the Rye. Apparently I missed that the first time I read the book. In "Shoeless Joe", Kinsella has Salinger discussing his various reasons for not wanting (rightfully) to be so engrossed in the public eye, and pleading to be left alone. At one point, he yells "I am not Holden Caulfield!", as many people may have claimed him to be in the past. I thought it was rather humerous the way Kinsella dispells myths about Mr. Salinger, while creating a whole new set of them with his character. Kinsella shows in "Shoeless Joe" that just because a person finds human society to be unworthy of his bother, he is neither a hermit or a mentally questionable recluse. I myself have felt as both Salinger, Holden, and many others have felt since the beginning of our society's creation. Why waste my time with this when there are so many other better ways to live my life? Why not quit my job and live in a cave amongst the wild? Why not leave school and build a simple cabin in the woods? Not many have had the courage to break the mold and the grip that society holds onto us so tightly with. I admire Salinger for doing something that most only dream of. Thank you.

   Sarah

   ❦

Dear J. D. Salinger,

Hey, J. D. do you remember the afternoons you, me, Perk, Spence and Bobby Greene used to spend in your place drinking beer and watching the sun set behind Mount Ascutney? Those were the days my friend. Man, there is an awful lot of misinformation about you on the web and that's too bad. I just found out today that Joyce Maynard (never heard of her) plans to write a memoir about her affair with you. To what end? Sounds like she plans to use your name to make a few buck for herself.

Do you remember my cousin Shirley who interviewed you in 1953? An article on the net says she was a 1-year old Windsor, Vermont High School girl. I mean, how may 1 year-old high school girls are there? Some of this stuff they're putting out on the "net" about you is just utterly ridiculous, as I'm sure you will agree. I often think of the good times we all had together in Windsor and Cornish and am glad to know that you are still able to maintain your privacy.

Bob Blaney

❧

Deah Mistah Salingah,

As a Southern Belle (though I was born in NH), a model, and someone who LOVES fame and all its accoutrements, no matter how vulgar or shallow, I'm somewhat mystified as to why I relate so well to your characters, your Glass family, and especially Zooey Glass. I didn't grow up in that kind of family. I'm not a spiritually well-versed twenty-something male. I'm not even alienated or malajusted like that little snot Caulfield. I've been thinking about it for years, and I've finally concluded that it's because you're SO FREAKING BRILLIANT you could make me relate to a whisk broom. Thanks for sharing this stuff, okay? And I promise that I'll never make a pilgrimage to your house.

Nicole Corrow

Dear J. D. Salinger,

Our English class is reading The Catcher In The Rye. Personally the book
is one of my top favorites of all time. One of the characters in this book
that I hate is Stradlater. He reminds me of one of my old friends that I
can't stand now. I used to like this girl named Kelly, and my friend Joe
actually asked her out, just too get on my nerves. I will never forget that
experience ever. I think that the fight scene between Holden and
Stradlater was very realistic. It relates to me in real life by that one day
when Joe came over my house right after he went out on a date with Kelly.
He had to drop off Kelly at home because it was getting late, and Kelly's
parents were real strict on how late she stayed out. When Joe was over my
house he didn't talk about the date at all. All he wanted to do was play
Sega. I always hated it when he sat there knowing that I wanted to know
what went on and not say a word about it. So finally I asked him if anything happened, but all he would do is look at the screen and play the day-
lights out of the Sega. So I told him that he is an idiot with no life, and
that he couldn't get a girl if his life depended on it. The next thing that I
knew was that I had an ice pack on my head and was lying on my coach.
Sometimes I feel like Holden in the way that he feels all by himself and
doesn't care about anyone. When my friends don't believe me of something and I am telling the truth, I just ignore them and go home. If you
don't mind I have some questions I want to ask you. Please write back
answering the questions:

1. What was going through your mind when the person that killed John
Lennon blamed the killing on your book?

2. Do you enjoy any other leisure than reading and writing books?

3. Do you play or happen to like any sports? If so, what sports?

4. Do you plan on writing any more books? If so, on what topic?

Thank you very much too use your time on reading my paper. If you can
write back I would be very surprised and amused, but if you can't then I
understand. I just like to mention that I do not like books that much, but

I have to admit The Catcher In The Rye is a very great book. When I read it, I can' t stop reading it. Any way thanks again and hope you have a nice day.

Sincerely,
John Solomos

❦

Dear J. D. Salinger,

The happiest moment in my entire life
(that I can remember) was listening to a story I think
was called "The Laughing Man". My boyfriend read it to me
while I sat sunning myself. The combination of the story,
and the sun, and probably our age was perfect. I think back
to that moment, it always makes me smile. Thank you.

Mary Plinzke

❦

Dear J. D. Salinger,

I just purchased another copy of Catcher in a disgusting, dusty antique shop in Pennsylvania. Don't get me wrong. This place was great. They had old tubs, toilets, and rusty bikes in the backyard, dozens of broken doors and windows in the side yard, yellow-edged black and white photographs of smiling lovey-dovey couples who must be so totally dead by now, and empty sticky bottles from products that no one makes anymore lined up on the window sill. I felt funny disturbing the neatly formed coating of dust that had collected so perfectly through the years on the crooked book-shelf. However, when I saw it, I just had to get a copy of "365 Ways to

Cook Hamburger" for my friend Jenn's bridal shower. (It went over well, and yes, I also got her something from Fortunoff's).

That's when I saw it. The Catcher.

Nice copy. It's from the 25th printing in April, 1963, and there's a picture of Holden on the cover. He's wearing that crazy hat, which for some reason, I thought had ear flaps, but it doesn't. There's a plug for Breakfast at Tiffany's inside, too, another Signet Book . . . "now a Paramount film starring Audrey Hepburn . . ." The book is exactly nine years older than me. The binding wasn't even wrinkled. The cover wasn't creased. No one had ever read it.

I had to buy it. Had to.

I dusted it off and saran-wrapped it, and I can't wait until I get married, have children, get old, die, and someone in my family coldly sells it to some other glorified junk dealer, who will probably be named Maurice. Just on purpose, I haven't read it either. Have a lovely day.

> *Sincerely,*
> *Orlie Grodzinski*

❦

Dear J. D. Salinger, Buddy Glass, et al.

As a child genius, myself, I have been naturally inclined to despise your work and your Glass family, hell, throw in the Caufield family as well, as an overmanipulated, self indulgent, boring, and otherwise unimportant portrait of yourself. In effect, this whole planet you have constructed does nothing but say that you, Mr. Salinger, are a fame crazy, super ego all too worried about changing the reflection in the mirror.

Ah, hell, I'm just kidding, J. D., I just needed some type of a ringer to start this nonsense off with. The thing with these unholy websites is that they are so directed at glorifing their subject that any criticism or negative-ness is shot down like an oversexed bull. In all honesty, you are a blessing to anyone cabable of reading the English language, and, in my years as a hack-trying-to-be-writer I can honestly say that you are one man I would feel very comfortable sitting at a bar with in complete silence. With that at hand,

Question one: The girl I desire desperately to marry is from your home-town, Cornish, NH, and, as things are in NH, her father works as a volun-teer fireman and has been inside your house. Imagine that. I'm sure only a finger full of people can claim that. Anyway, I know, bygonne, that all these years you have been no stranger to the typewriter — or is it word processor these days, God don't say its so — and I've heard that you have tucked away very comfortably in a vault, or some other safekeeping device, three finished books, or collections, or work of some sort. Well, anyway, I'm wondering that if I offered, very humbly and without expectation of any sort, if I offered you a cheap bottle of Chianti and a new snow shovel, a really good one, that you would release whatever it is that is encarcerated for us, your overzelous and admiring readers? I promise to make good on my side of the arrangment. A bottle of chianti and a shovel, plus a chance to see the hometown of my dreamed-wife-to-be. And, of course, to drink a glass with you — I promise not to wear a hunting hat.

Question Two: Do you have a corkscrew or should I bring one?

Question Three: I know it has to be hell on Earth to be J. D. Salinger, but I do have one other question that kind of has, in a way, a lot to do with J. D. Salinger and your chosen reclusivity. I once had a teacher in college, only a few years ago as it is, that said that if Neitzsche had know the conse-quences of his writings that he would have in no way ever published. Not to compare you with N., any comparison of living human beings is to me completely unnatural and pointless. But, if you could forsee the conse-quence of Catcher, that is, before you wrote it, would you have? If you hadn't all us poor saps would be without, but you would have a chance to live in society, New York even, without Mark David Chapmans and others clinging to your words like Dogma. Not to make light of Lennon, he is always missed. But, could you forsee this riotous following? If you did, why make such a big deal over your fame? If you didn't, then would you change anthing? I guess that's more than one question — yes, I also hate people who ask more than one question and then say I guess that's more than one question — but it's something that I've been wondering for awhile.

Darren Ursino

💌

Dear J. D. Salinger,

I'm from SPAIN and here unfotunately we doesn't read your books too much.
I have read "THE CATHCHER IN THE RYE" just because of one of my teachers was wrong and put it into the list of books we have to read in summer.
Since that day I have read all your books, "The great Gagtby" and a little of Ring Ladner.
Thank you for telling me there's more people like me.
If anyone who love "THE CATCHER IN THE RYE" is reading this, please write to me.
I just have question for the best american and universal writer of all the times:
WHY DOESN'T HOLDEN CALLED JANE?
Sorry for my bad english.
Please write me people!!!!!

Ester Manzano S.

Greetings Mr. Salinger

If you do happen to read this for some unknown reason, I was wondering what style of beer do you like? I personally prefer pale ales and stouts.

Oh yeah, I also enjoyed your writings — right there with Ginsberg, Bukowski, Burroughs and the gang. You definitely caught the true unabridged attitude of postwar Americans.

Eternally,
Russ

🦋

Dear J. D. Salinger,

I would like to tell the World of a wonderful new experience which can only be attributed to reading the works of Salinger from start to finish over and over again and again—> I have found that after about 5 or 6 complete readings the reader (in this case me, JOHNNY fAME!!, also known as the greatest entertainer in history) begins to experience some quite wild and fanciful effects of "psycho-delia" and mental abstractions, much similar to the sensation of falling into a void of endless color with glowing substances flowing across your naked body like a particularly sheer and transparent type of mucus (hey I've never used that word before!) or even perhaps more like rubbery intestinal fluids — but anyway they slide across all parts of your naked body (even the personal areas) and then you continue to fall, fall, fall into a heaping pile of mushy nothingness but which yet has texture even though it is nothing; Also after regaining conciousness of your actual reality and cleaning yourself off like a cat you then have a sensation of a total glorious numbness and when you realize this you boil a pot of water to the point of bubbles on TOP of bubbles and so then pour it on your hand because it's so easy now that you are numb. Then later when you are getting your perscription filled at the Drug Place where they keep all the narcotics and chemicals in a big jar with a lock on it so nobody can find out about the secret powers of the universe, all of a sudden you begin to have what's known as a "Flashback" and there you are, falling through a colorful, gushy void of almost clear substances into a giant pile of soft nothingness and it begins again and repeats twice. The whole thing is really a mind-opener and then when you go to the computer machine to send your message into the magical electronic world inside you begin to notice that the skin is growing back on to your hand. But then you realize that there are little people living inside your hand and they are sticking needles in and out of all of your pores and so you smash it with the nearest heavy object which in this case was an electronic Bread Toaster. So I thank you now as I have to go take some more pills, but I am encouraging you all to use heartily your God-given ability to read, read, read and indeed read to each other.

Thank you everybody; I love people.

JOHNNY fAME!!

❦

Dear J. D. Salinger,

hello!!!!!!!!!!!!!!!!!! We do not think you'll ever read this letter, but if you do we just want you to know that we love your book. We know what the press says about u, and we agree what u r doing because we know what you are doing. We know what you are doing!!!!!!!!!!!!!! i reapeat we know what u r doing

Dear J. D. Salinger,

i hate you i have to write an essay on your collabortion of bad words called catcher in the rye. i will fail because of your miserable book. u have ruined my education and i will not get to uni because of u. i hope ur happy. dont write anymore please.

> *yours hatingly from the collection of holden haters.*
> *filip*

❧

Dear J. D. Salinger,

I am 15 years old, and I just started reading Catcher in the Rye. I have one question, why do you use the words "goddamn" so much? You use the words on like practically every page. The words don't bother me, i'm just curious as to why you use them in sentences that don't even need swearing.

> *Ryan*

❧

Thank you for Seymour.

> *Geeti*

❧

Dear J. D. Salinger,

Wazzup nigga. How's Cornish this time of year? New York is fine, also. Please excuse me for assuming you're not a real hermit and that you do keep in touch with some closer acquaintances. Some people make it seem as if you're totally cut off. I guess meeting new people must be a little strange when you assume they've read your book. A lot of paranoids, schizophrenics and the socially paralytic choose to become celebrities instead of going to the trouble of introducing themselves at parties. Are you any of those things? Probably you are, but you're pretending to be an important and famous writer instead. Don't you think it's a little bit pretentious to make such a big deal about not publishing any more? You chose to publish in the first place, and you wouldn't be nearly as famous if you didn't fight it so much. You probably wouldn't admit to getting off on the reaction to your first book. Not to mention the cash and the ho's. You're not the Dalai Lama and you're not Oprah. She's a chunky black woman on TV, which I doubt you watch any more. You can't make yourself unfamous. Cough it up. Either publish everything you've got left in you or hurry up and die. That's about all I wanted to say. Drop me a line if you're coming through the city.

> Sincerely,
> Dan Paton.

❦

Dear J. D. Salinger,

I am a sophomore in high school and I was assigned to read Catcher In The Rye. I am sorry but I somewhat don't understand it.

> Anonymous

❦

Ha Salinger, you think you got fan mail bad off. Well you got it easy, my name is Micael Bolton. How much does that suck.

> Lovingly,
> Micael, no . . . not the Micael Bolton

Dear J. D. Salinger,

After reading The Catcher In The Rye three times now I've become an
angry existentialist. Society disgusts me. Even this very internet page is all
just set up probably to make money. If I write a book I'm not going to let
anyone make any money out of it. I'll give it out for free. I keep getting
blamed by my family for not revising hard for exams. There are only two
subjects I want to pass, english and music, as they're the only ones that
don't involve getting phoney jobs where you have to be polite to everyone.
I'm sick of this world.

Is Holden growing up? is all the "falling" meaning into childhood? Is Jane
a symbol of his childhood that he never seems to get back, because he's
going into the diseased world of Adulthood?

I spoke to someone else who's read Perfect day for Bananafish and they
thought Seymour was a pervert. I think he's a kindly man who's disgusted
with the world and couldn't bear it knowing the girl would probably grow
up. That's the thing about nowadays. You can't get a nice man tickling a
little girl without morons turning their heads and expecting him at any
minute to rape her.

If society sorted itself out no-one would have to be robbing places to make
livings. Hell Is Other People.

    Laurie Bichan

    ❦

Dear J. D. Salinger,

I just finished watching the pt anderson film "magnolia" and I could not
stop thinking about how much it reminded me of your works. Not only in
subject, but mostly in style and I thought "what a wonderful thing, that
such an original style has been adapted to film." It turns out that I was
right, after a small amount of research I found that mr. anderson is heavily

influenced by you (i think he wants to be you). So thank you for inspiring such a great film, and thank you for all of your works they remind me, I'm not crazy.

Brian Cantrell

❦

Hey Salinger.

What's goin' on? Do you think that you could possibly move next door to me and write a story for me every day like you have nothing better to do? I guess not. Anywho, have a good life.

Thom Luther C.

❦

Dear J. D. Salinger,

Reading through this guestbook, is it any wonder why Salinger keeps to himself? Some of you folks have some very serious issues that you must work out with yourself. If I had rude, obnoxious jerks trying to contact me saying that my book was crap, I don't think I'd be accommodating to the public either. Not everybody here, but a lot . . .

Not necessarily J. D.'s reason, but it would surely be mine. 'Tis the reason why all my work goes unpublished . . . for me to read, and me alone . . . after all, who could relate more? Does it really matter what a bunch of Internet psychos or literary critics think? Writing is expression. Simple as that.

If you don't like Salinger's writing, I dare say that you're not in touch with a part of yourself, deep down inside. It's not Salinger's problem. It's yours.

Respectfully,
Anonymous

Dear J. D. Salinger,

you're small in the pants

🦋

Dear J. D. Salinger,

I came to read your book, The Catcher In The Rye, through a dear friend
of mine. He was someone with a terrific sense of humor and I couldn't figure out, for the life of me, why he would want to engross himself in a classic. Naive as I was, I mistook The Catcher In The Rye for being just
another boring piece of required literature. Incidentally, my friend offered
to let me read a passage out of his copy that he was convinced would
change my mind. He was right, it did. However, soon after reading that
small portion of your book, actually going to the library and checking it
out escaped my mind (as many things do.) Later, that same year, my dear
friend died in a horrible traffic accident. In my grief, I remembered The
Catcher In The Rye and, to be close to him, I checked out that very same
copy and read it cover to cover. As I read, my tears turned to laughter and
back to tears again. I didn't realize it before he passed, because I never
took the time to read your book before then, but Holden Caulfield seemed
to be the mirror image of my friend. Not in his physical appearance or in
his experiences, but in his personality. Therefore, that book has always
been exceptionally special to me, and not simply for the reason of appreci-
ating it's literary value, but also admiring the way you seemed to capture a
thousand souls in one character.

S. Wilson

TWIMC,

There has never been any ambivalence in the behaviour of JDS. He has always, and will always want to be seen as a recluse. I'm deeply curious to know the answer to this question: Is his reclusion (1.) truly the result of a psychological problem, neurosis if you will, or (2.) willingly and knowingly self imposed to achieve the desired publicity effect?

Of course there can be no certain answer until JDS passes on. Statistically speaking, I suspect that will occur before 2010. Things will change then, and the public will be allowed to read whatever he's been working on for 50 years.

Which begs the question, why be a writer if you, by choice, have no readers? JDS has always been about contradictions, which is why my belief is that the answer to the first question is (2.)

He's a media animal. A minimalist who believes that as long as he's living well and comfortably there is no reason to exert himself. He's creating an icon, and he's smart enough to know it.

This message is not so much to JDS himself. That would be unrealistic. I do hope that his readers will read this and see that the myth is just a man.

   H. Denee

Hey big S, if its allright to call ya that, i figured ya wouldn't mind seeing as how a name isn't really a representation at all of who or what we are, but of course thats something you taught me. First off as a 16 year old male reading your book i was almost appalled (not the strongest of spellers, unless of course that is correct, then that statement is retracted) that you allowed it to be printed with a white paper cover. Now don't get me wrong, i appreciate as much as the next guy saving a buck or two, i'd happily pay more for it, but those two dollars were better spent supporting the corporations of america. At any rate, some of us have been plagued since birth with naturally sweaty hands, and from it i nearly blackened the cover of your most famous read. I'm sure you've never struggled with that but now when i try to share it with others (just a passage or two, i'd never loan the book out, wouldn't steal from ya) they are more disgusted. May i request that if you ever find the time to release another book or you publish something new that you keep the paper cover but possibly make it black, or heck, grey may even fit better, thats really your preferance, but if it were mine it'd be something that dirty finger prints won't show on. Anyway, i've no criticism, i'm sure after you released it there must have been something you'd like to have changed, or at least i always look back and feel that way towards . . . well . . . history essay's, or something else that doesn't hold my interest. Good life to you sir.

~Ron

❦

Dear J. D. Salinger,

Do you watch the sunsets?

TANIA b

❦

Dear J. D. Salinger,

I know you're going to think I made this up, but it's true. My name is Katie, I am sixteen years old. When I was young, I was called "gifted" even a "child genius". My parents were thrilled, and I was put through rigorous schooling. It sounds like such a cliche, but my grades were great, my IQ tests were even better, and all I wanted was a friend. At the age of eight in

my high-school level literature course, we read, "Catcher In the Rye." That book became my friend whilst other young people were too intimidated to speak to me. On a frequent basis, according to my parents and teachers, I began to refer to Holden "as though he were a real person". (Their words; he IS a real person, to me). I guess I got kind of burned out by the time I was thirteen and a senior in high school. Everything was very hectic; I had gotten reccomendations to Oxford and Harvard, among other universities, and everybody was absolutely thrilled. But, that year I flunked out. I had reached rock bottom, just like Holden. I took a few months off and started afresh; now, I am a freshman at Princeton University. I guess I'm one of the "phonies", but I'll never forget the courage you and Holden (and the Glass family and Esme and the Laughing Man and, if we're talking about fictional characters, I might as well throw in some other favorites, Jamie Tyrone and T. S. Garp and J. Alfred Prufrock), gave me, and still give me. Thank you for listening to my "whole godamn autobiography", and for writing your wonderful books. To slightly misquote the film, "How Green Was My Valley": "Men like you can never die. They remain forever alive in the flames of memory. How green was my valley, then."
Thank you.

Katie Marlow

❦

Dear J. D. Salinger,

While other books for teenagers are all about popularity and sex, you are the one author who understands feeling depressed, lonely, a failure, and angry. Thank you for epitomizing the TRUE feelings of youth.

Michelle Marlon

Dear J. D. Salinger,

I just want to start out this letter by saying that I hate hero worship, I think it is anti-American. I don't understand why people drool over you, to be honest. If I were you, I'd be a bit scared. I don't understand a lot of your books. As a student of psychology, I can say that Holden Caulfield is mentally ill. I think all of your "sweet little girl" characters are quite creepy and Lolita-esque. I don't think a young girl with a blossoming sexuality would go up to an older man, a soldier no less, simply because "he looked so lonely." I don't understand what motivated Seymour's suicide. The fact that the little girl would grow up? Growing up is a beautiful process, one that he obviously never experienced. You have a true affinity for writing about clinically depressed and troubled New Yorkers, but your other talents are few, I'm sorry to say.

> *Annette*

❦

Hi Mr. Salinger,

I would like to ask two questions of you —
1) How are you doing today?
2) What did one wall say to the other wall?

> *Cordially,*
> *Andrew Topel*

❦

Dear J. D. Salinger,

Is Holden him or me or us?

> *Pete Floman*

Dear J. D. Salinger,

Just a little something that might be of interest to you. In my senior
Honors English class, we were discussing everything we had read in the
last four years. As you can probably guess, the unanimous favorite of all of
the literature was, "Catcher In the Rye." Our teacher posed a question:
What do you think happened to Holden Caulfied? Well, please correct me
if I'm wrong, but I think I've found the answer: After Holden flunked out,
he attended another pirvate school. Although his grades were less than
stellar, he attended Princeton University (you know how that sort of thing
works). He went on to recieve a law degree (after all, as he said himself,
"those boys really haul it in,"), but knew all along that his heart wasen't in
it. It was, by then, the late 50's to early 60's, and Holden had begun to
hang out with a group of young intellectuals (such as Abbie Hoffman),
and the seeds of revolution in Holden's life were firmly planted. But, as I
said before, that whole lawyer thing didn't fly, so he became a free-lance
writer (we knew all along that this was the course he would follow; he was
fated, perhaps doomed to, because of his deep sense of injustice and
knowledge of human nature.) Around this time, he married a nice young
woman (perhaps Jewish) and they had two young daughters. But, the 'ol
wife kinda took a backseat in those crazy 1960's years. Although he was a
bit old to be a student, he helped found Students for a Democratic
Society. He spent a summer in the company of Ken Kesey and his Merry
Pranksters, dropping acid in Haight-Ashbury. His wife (a very conventional
type who Holden married because of her crazy little habits; perhaps reminiscent of how Jane Gallagher kept all her kings in the back row?), left
him, taking their two little girls. Holden was heartbroken. Although he was
sometimes inattentive, he loved his wife and daughters very much and
couldn't live without them. His wife ended up divorcing him, but he got
full custody of the little girls (whose names were Viola and Iris). He was
still, of course, writing those free-lance articles, except they were turning
into books. (Published under an alias). He was making a good-sized
amount of money, and his love for the revolution had died out (although
there are certain 1960's movies I'm almost positive he wrote; for instance,

listen to the dialouge in "Easy Rider." Pure Holden.) For respectibility's sake, he returned to practicing law. This was the mid 1970's, and he was in his forties. Iris and Viola left for college. He took up with a very lovely younger woman, a writer, and he permenantly gave up the bar and returned to being a scribe. I picture him now as an old man sitting in his country home in Vermont. I think he still writes under an alias. Thank you for listening!

Audrey

☙

Dear J. D. Salinger,

If you were to make a movie poster out of The Catcher in the Rye what would you choose as a picture?

Melat

☙

Dear J. D. Salinger,

What can anybody say about a book they only half get? Critics can talk forever and go into great detail about how this means this and so on. I don't know if any of it is true, but mabey you don't want to give all the answers. Mystery tends to draw people away from the norm. But anyway, as I can't write vulgar things because God knows you never did, I'll really begin my letter because it's about time. About The Catcher in the Rye. Beep. You just turned off. The book is great about showing exactly how people think. But the one part in the book that explains what's what really is confusing. When he tells Pheobe about what he wants to be, is he trying to say that he wants to save all the other people in the book or that he just wants to save the children from seeing the world? Or is he trying to tell the reader don't be like the other characters or don't be like himself? In any case, I think he wants to save the world but can't, so he figures there's no point in doing anything and beig phony about it. The truth is, not every time someone smiles it's phony and he mabey sees that at the end. What made me interested is that I recently have this thought cross my mind that mabey God does't help everyone because they just ask and nothing ever happens. I mean, they might just stare out of their window and go places but nothing good happens, and if it does, they can't see it. They could be ignored and have a horrible life and can't deal with it. Is that why people kill other people in school shootings? Or do they have a brain problem and why would that happen? Did nobody help them? Will they go to Hell? I know you probably don't have the answers but at least I asked

Amanda

🦋

Dear J. D. Salinger,

I have read Catcher in the Rye with a lot of interest dude. I wish that I have a gramps like you man. I really wonder how you managed to use all those terms back then that doesn't even sound antique today. And Are You Alive? I don't hear jack about you. Why do u want to keep yourself under the hat man? For all I know, reading your book, I had a whale of a time. It kept me in there. I don't really relish reading, but your story was different, I just could not let it go amigo.

I do have to blame u though, for getting your ass kicked by Maurice. If I were you, I would have kicked HIS ass. Why you got to get socked then taken your money away?

You should not have been so yellow man. Yea, school does suck man. One minute. I thought in the book you said you would not go to the ivy but I see that you did, you attended Columbia. What is up wit' that? Well J. D.

you take care man. It's good to know you are famous round the world. Some friends of mine that are foreign are well aware of u and are in love with you. I will cruise J. D. Peace out, by by old J. D.

^.^

Jake Huntamire

🦋

Dear J. D. Salinger,

I noticed you used the phrase "estatically happy" in Seymore: an Introduction four times. The tattered copy I so precociously carry around im my back pocket and the "inspiring" underlined passages proves what an undying (I refrain from using FAN) follower I am. You inspired me at the ripe old age of thirteen to become the "estatically happy writer" I knew was inside. Thank You, Mr. Salinger, for the gift you've given me is invaluable.

Keisha

🦋

Dear J. D. Salinger,

Hey, Bob. I don't think that you should do any "Major League" movies anymore, but I did enjoy your run on "Mr. Belvadere." I'm glad you wrote "Catcher in the Rye." It's a great book and what people fail to realize is that you should be able to be completely comical and slapstick and still be taken seriously when you have something serious to say. For those of you out there reading this that don't know, J. D. Salinger is actual "Bob Uecker" who was a pro baseball player and was a "catcher." Yeah, I know it's hard to believe, but go check out his autobiography at the www.imdb.com and look up Bob Uecker. I've seen it many other places as well, it's the truth. Just remember, it's still the same book and is still as good and real as it was before you knew that a "funny man" from TV wrote it. Give him his due, he is/was what you thought JD Salinger was . . .

Joe

🦋

Dear Mr. Salinger,

I just wanted to let you know that I'm not going to read your daughter's memoir. Your books and stories have kept me sane, and the least I owe you is a little privacy.
Sincerely,

Christy Stockard

🦋

Dear J. D. Salinger,

I have learned after reading some books written about you that you have feet comprised, at least in part, of clay.

The authors of these books have tarred you with the brush of imperfection, which is, in these times, a venal sin. They have made their case that you are human, that you even have warts. Not such a big deal in itself, but the unwritten implication is that because you are flawed, so is your work.

That is why I am writing you this letter. To say it isn't so. To say that I don't care about your feet. They interest me no more than the feet of Faulkner, Fitzgerald or Steinbeck, all of which contained ample amounts of clay. What matters to me is the words, the insights, the characters that you have created.

Your work will outlive your feet.

Thank you for Franny, Teddy, Holden and the others who touched that place in many of us that, until they touched it, we didn't even know was there.

John Patterson

❦

Dear Mr. Salinger,

It's a little after midnight now, where I live, and I will not lie. I found this site while searching, in vain you may be pleased to note, for illegal copies of your works. As much as I would like to respect your demand for privacy, the kitten side of me, the writer side of me, is eager to devour any work of yours I can find, and as soon as I finish this letter I will return to my search.

I read Catcher In The Rye in school, like a billion other students, and groaned at when every time I turned a page there was another. Something about being assigned a book really takes all the fun out of reading it. And to be honest, it was very likely that I would never pick up another of your books again. Even today Catcher In The Rye is not my favorite, although now I do appreciate it more than then.

I did not return to your works until last December. As a writer-in-progress I make it my duty to ask any person upon introduction, their favorite book. Last December, I found myself at one of those parties everyone has been to . . . lots of people you don't want to know, most of them at their worst, loud music, more smoke than oxygen. I was the youngest there, and definetly not the social butterfly. In an attempt to salvage the rest of my evening, I escaped to the kitchen, where I happened upon a man in his mid twenties named Andrew. Andrew, whose last name I shall omit, was a traveling novelist, stuck in this dry desert where I live for the next seven months while he built up the finances to move on. Although now he is gone and I have lost contact, while he was here I milked him shamelessly for all the writing advice I could, driven on, I will admit, by a slight attraction. And during our brief friendship, he said that the book that made him want to become a writer was Nine Stories, by none other than yourself.

I went to the only bookstore in town and bought a copy, in the meantime running into the little yellow edition of, wait, what is this, notes on Catcher In The Rye???? I resisted the urge to write "read the book" in big bold letters on the inside cover and merely turned away.

After Nine Stories, nothing could keep me away. I read your other works, Franny being my all time favorite, and your mastery of the language and of the nature of human beings has changed the way I write. Although I realize that the chances of you actually reading this letter are zip I wish to thank you for what you have published, for what you have given of yourself to the world and to people like me who are devoting their lives to the love of literature and the desire to produce characters that will be remembered. My dearest best friend Randy, who is also an aspiring (and very talented) writer and I intended, at one point, to tour the U.S. and visit all the graves of those who's writing we cherished. (Unfortunately, the majority are deceased) Though we currently lack the finances (and by he way, if its any comfort a copy of the stolen uncollected works goes for something around $750.00 and UP, so I will probaby never get my dirty little hands on any of it) when we do get going you are on our list of writers we aspire to be like, and whether you are alive or have passed on we will leave lilly's on your doorstep to let you know that we were there, and we appreciate what of yourself you have given us.

> *With Sincerity,*
> *Jennifer Kay*
> *17 years old*
> *Arizona*

Dearest Jerry,

I fear that today will be dreadfully boring; I have nothing to keep myself
occupied tonight and socializing with my roommates has been little more
than a nuisance as of late. I purchased William Carlos Williams' autobiography the other day, because I was bored and it was a lot simpler than wad-
ing through a whole lot of "Contemporary Literature". Mr. Williams and
I share a birthday.

Not that it's a matter of concern at all, but it's raining a bit outside; the first
rain that I've seen in about a month and a half . . . It has the same deaden-
ing effect on me, which is both pleasant and aggravating. Pleasant because
it acts as wine, dulling the edges a bit, numbing me . . . Aggravating because I'm to be cooped up in my room, reading or on the telephone with
my mother.

Perhaps I'll have a cigarette out of my window tonight.

I'm moving soon, with Jeffrey; I don't think you've met him yet, but he has
compatible taste in architecture and design. You're more than welcome to
drop in when we're settled . . . It would allow you the opportunity to meet
Kayla, whom I'm sure you'd be charmed to meet.

> *Warmest Regards,*
> *Jay Watts*
> *Victoria, BC*

❦

Dear J. D. Salinger,
I am the chief editor for a spiritual magazine called the Rays of the
Harmonist. It is published in Vrindavana, India bi-monthly. I was sur-
prised to find that you have had a deep interest in Vedanta for years. I am
involved with Bhakti Vedanta, that is, Vedanta which concludes in Bhakti.
I really doubt if you would be interested in corresponding on these matters

for any great length of time, due to your elderly age and privacy. But I missed regretfully writing to some very important writers in the past before it was too late, like Borges and Ginsberg. I would like to know if it is at all possible to understand why you do not go further and understand the Bhakti side of Vedanta and not the Advaita side, since Advaita culminates in annihilation of the self and impersonalism. How has this influenced your life in the aspects of writing? I dare to say that probably Holden Cauldfield and the rest of your characters have that wring of nihilistic voidism in them . . . I have not read Catcher in the Rye since college and afterwards I began my spiritual search through mantra-yoga or bhakti-yoga. Is it at all possible to get any word from you on your viewpoint about Advaita Vedanta? I would also like to send you some of our magazines that have been published. Please allow the courtesy of some reply to my quest as I am interested in your spiritual quest even more than your writings.

> *Yours in the service of bhakti-devi,*
> *Tirthapada Das*

❧

Dear J. D. Salinger,

You are an irrate octupus that inks away at the bottom of the sea . . . Such a clever mollusk . . you got these clams sighing in awe . . all tucked in their limp bivalve beds . . covered in the brine of existence . . . So go find your- self a cave . . and leave the eels to their mud.

> *Crystallyn Drischel*

❧

Dear J. D. Salinger,

how come you eat only organic food?

Dear People,

I thought I should point out that J. D. Salinger does not read these letters. He doesn't know you, nor does he care about you; he shouldn't have to. Furthermore, stop getting so excited over his books, particularly "Catcher in the Rye." They are books; that is all. His books may contain clever ideas or be well-written, but many other works of literature have these same attributes (Oscar Wilde's "The Picture of Dorian Gray," for example). You may be able to relate to the characters in his books; this is because they are human, like you. You are not the only one to claim to have a "revelation" after reading "Catcher in the Rye." You are not the first person to praise Salinger's writing, nor will you be the last. Finally, don't start out your letter with disclaimers. Stop humbling yourself (or boasting about yourself, for that matter); it just makes you look ignorant. This is a fault.

   Matt Mitchell

dear matt mitchell:

how exactly does one know that mister salinger doesn't read these letters? perhaps he doesnt, but i dont believe you know him personally enough to make that particular statement. i think it's absolutely wonderful that people "get excited" over his books, it's excellent when an author writes in such a way that a reader can become attached to his work and feel a sort of personal assurance in them. you're correct when you said that we understand the characters in his literature solely because they are human, but this is why salinger is essentially such a marvelous author — he doesn't dodge the fact that his stories should have imperfections or truths in them. unlike so many other popular novels of the day, his stories don't stray away from the fact that "reality bites" and life isnt a basket of flowers at all times. im sorry that i couldnt personally address you (as you've left no sign of an email), but your preferences dont include the rest of the world's, which i hope you've learned by now.

rebecca

❧

Dear J. D. Salinger

You rock man! I've just finished reading "Raise High the Roof Beam, Carpenters" and "Seymour: An Introduction." In fact, I skipped my Anatomy lecture just so I could finish reading it. And finishing reading it was no mean feat, with about a million medical students interupting me every second! And when I say a million, I mean just one very persistent boy. I was just sitting outside the lecture theater, reading, absorbed, when he came up to me and started telling me about wall to wall carpeting. (God knows why!) And I was like, whatever. Then he snatched the book out of my hands and said "whatyareadn?" To tell you the truth I didnt really like him touching the book. Its not like its a bible to me or anything. But it still felt wrong. Anyway, I had a hard time trying to convince him that it was fiction. Possibly because of the footnotes. He had never heard of it or you. I was shocked, shocked. Then he said "oh, its the guy that wrote The Catcher in the Rye"

"YES!" I almost yelled, "Yes it is!! Have you read it??!!" Finally, a friend in medicine!! Thank god!! No more spending my time in between labs alone, all alone.

Except that he was like "No, i just read that off the front of the book."

Gutted.

It was sort of amusing and depressing at the same time that he had never heard of you or your classic. He continued to molest the book, turning it around like it was some puzzle, possibly a rubix cube, that could be solved by looking at it from different angles. Him: "this doesnt look like a fiction book, it looks like the kind of book you read in an English class."

Me: "Yeah, a good book." but I said it quietly, so as not to offend.

We then went on to talk about numerous other things, such as how a vasectomy is "the perfect operation".

He also remarked upon the fact that I was wearing a lot of make-up. Which was strange, but I suppose observant of him. Or possibly rude. He had really bad pimply skin, but I didnt remark on that. Why do other people feel the need to point out your physical flaws and characteristics? Just the other day some people remarked that I was "a stick". I suppose because I am a girl, I am suppost to take it as a veiled compliment of sorts, but it annoys the hell out of me anyway. You know how Zooey says that he wishes everyone in the world looked the same? So do I.

Anyway, thankfully it was time for the lecture, but I decided to just stay where I was sitting outside and finish reading. Anyway I wont ramble on for much longer, but if you are reading this, I just want to thank you for teaching me something important. "Seymour once said that all we do our whole lives is go from one little piece of holy ground to the next". It kind of helped me to realize that just because someone is a tactless pimply guy who has never heard of J. D. Salinger, you shouldnt hate them for it. Lots of people think that the message behind your books is one of exclusion and shunning people who are "phoney" or "corny" (or science geeks who have never read a book in their lives). But, for me, its really the opposite. Its about valueing and respecting people because they are all your brothers and sisters, they are all "the fat lady". So thank you for helping my days at med school to be a little less bitter and acrimonious.
You're cool, stay cool

Alex Gordon

Dear J. D. Salinger,

A lot of people around here have read Sallinger. Boy, what a signature of
appreciation. With a lot of bad grammar and spelling. Sorry. These days!
This isn't really to old J. D. since soon he's going to be dead and before
that he's not going to read even any book of letters published off the old
web. What I mean is, the fellow is going to die soon, and if your soul is
made of a bunch of words and a few images, all these letters are going to
rankle in his soul like so many big bloodthirsy mosquitos swarming the
ankles of a bull elephant, who will never really "feel" the insects, but will
nevertheless be a little annoyed at them, maybe he'll blink. So, there are
all these words swarming around, but they're trapped in this black box. So
I'll just let a couple of them live for a minute: 1) I think the best letter
posted on here is by one "ddickers": I'm going to write her personally too
just because I'm a go-getter and I don't care about thanks. She wrote a
damn good letter. And 2) I'd like to share a little living Sallinger with the
listening audience (it is concerned, of course, with absolute immitation,
but maybe that's where it all starts) and I'm not going to give anything
away with titles and so on. I used to work in an opera house and one night
I had the peculiar job of the elevator boy, where you greet people coming
in push the button for them. Not many people came in that night and
the elevator had no light coming from the outside world and I was reading
J. D. and starting to feel sensorially deprived and, in fact, was, and got to
this one peculiar part of a story just before the end when the elevator doors
swung open. I immediately took my shoes and socks off, but the people
still got on, though somewhat taken aback it seemed to me. Then I just
stood there and went through the whole routine (because a lady that
boarded was looking at my bare white feet): "Ma'am, are you looking at
my feet?" All she said was no. "Well, if you are, it's alright, you know." And
all she said was no I wasn't looking at your feet. I forebore with the swearing, not because I don't appreciate a good blue streak here and there, but
because I was a little scared, and said, "Look, just don't take a sneaky look,
go ahead, get a look, I mean I like my feet too, even though they're so

white." Then she asked her husband or whoever he was if they could please get off. Anyway, there is so much criticism and it makes me tired and that dickers did write a good letter.

ben shook

Postscript

The Changing Art of
Critical Response to the
Fiction of J. D. Salinger

Will Hochman

J. D. Salinger is about as likely to discuss his writing craft on national television as he is to respond to any of the letters in this book. But *Letters to
J. D. Salinger* is not intended for Salinger so much as it is intended to
advance understanding of both traditional and new ways of responding
to literature. Critics, with an interest in Salinger's fiction or a curiosity
about his withdrawal from public life, have produced thousands of pages
of writing. But those intent on developing their interpretations of
Salinger's prose and increasing their understanding of his life often over-
look the point that Salinger's writing has made the world of literature into
a more humane place for readers. The contributors to *Letters to J. D.
Salinger* show how literature *works* by explaining how Salinger's fiction
encourages readers to become writers and helps students and teachers to
become more compassionate thinkers.

Letters to J. D. Salinger works in so many creative and wonderful ways
that even J. D. Salinger might enjoy it. This book illustrates new modes of
interaction among readers, critics, and authors that reader-response theo-
rists have developed in order to explore a more complete literary spectrum
of readers responding to an author's work. *Letters to J. D. Salinger* shows
readers "talking" critically and creatively to an author. Don De Grazia's
letter relates how Salinger's books inspired a creative student to mature
into a dedicated writer. And teachers work with students every day to help
produce the literary insights that *Letters to J. D. Salinger* illustrates. But
the fact of the matter is that too often we think of literature as something
beyond ourselves when it's really about the ideas that grow inside of us.

Letters to J. D. Salinger brings together a group of very diverse readers, crystallizing critical and creative thinking into a book that synthesizes and celebrates Salinger's literary effects.

One can imagine that literature is a constant invitation to its readers and writers, though criticism has argued for ages about just what this invitation means. One of my favorite explanations about how literature works comes from Louise Rosenblatt, one of the earliest practitioners of reader-response criticism. In her 1978 book, *The Reader, the Text, the Poem,* she writes: "Under the magnetism of the ordered symbols of the text, [the reader] marshals his resources and crystallizes out from the stuff of memory, thought, and feeling a new order, a new experience, which he sees as the poem. This becomes part of the ongoing stream of his life experience, to be reflected on from any angle important to him as a human being." Rosenblatt understands literature to be an event in time that involves a transactional process between reader, text, and writer. This event then becomes part of the reader's life experience. Rosenblatt's transactional theory of literature *as exploration* begins to explain much of what readers really experience.

Though the spirit and meaning of Salinger's words may have helped some of us change the literary worlds we want to inhabit, it's doubtful that Salinger's writing could be so effective without literary merit. Books by Eberhard Alsen, Warren French, Gerald Rosen, Elizabeth Kurian, Sanford Pinsker, John Wenke, and many others have defined Salinger's achievement in traditional critical terms. Some of these seasoned Salinger critics have also contributed to *Letters to J. D. Salinger,* perhaps because they believe Salinger's work is among the most important writing of our time or perhaps because they understand the wisdom of connecting with as many readers as possible *as readers themselves.*

The interest in Salinger's work has withstood tests of time and of heart, but the literary world we know now is changing. Every book, indeed every published word changes what literature is. The world of criticism is changing as well. Janet Malcolm, in the June 21, 2001, issue of the *New York Review of Books*, questions some of the past critical responses to Salinger and suggests that different interpretations of Salinger's work are necessary. Malcolm, for example, does not agree with John Updike about the "separate Frannys in *Franny and Zooey*. But the critical changes Malcolm calls for may be larger than simply reevaluating interpretations. She asserts a need to reevaluate Salinger because he continues to affect so many readers in emotional ways that critics hesitate to fully analyze and explore.

Letters to J. D. Salinger will help readers understand themselves in contexts that are more human than critical, while simultaneously exposing readers to some of the most important critical ideas of Salinger's work that scholars have been writing about for the past fifty years. As a teacher, I've tried to show my students that writers shouldn't seem to be *about* something, they must *be* it . . . with their words. When this book was proposed I had my students read a letter I wrote to Salinger. My students knew that I was trying to make an almost impossible reader-writer connection in that letter since it was well known that Salinger didn't respond to strangers. So they helped me focus on simply making my concerns about Internet copyright explicit and concise. Later, when Chris Kubica asked me to help him with *Letters to J. D. Salinger,* I read in hundreds of submissions first-rate evidence that my appreciation of Salinger's compassionate and insightful impact is widely shared. Salinger's writing has helped thousands of readers, writers, teachers, and students experience literature beyond the confines of schools and critical essays. And that may be what is most important and most misunderstood about his work. The response to Salinger's fiction is advancing beyond literary analysis and is now making important critical inroads.

As one who wrote his dissertation on Salinger, and now as a contributor to this book, I realize that focusing only on scholarly responses limits literary understanding. The power of Salinger's work is that it has consistently presented great storytelling, dialogue, and characterization while enabling millions of readers to see themselves in new and better ways. Perhaps it is the love, compassion, and understanding in Salinger's words that make so many readers begin to see the fiction they read as an invitation to become writers. This is why the writer Frederick Busch thanks Salinger for teaching him to "risk emotion" and to "dare to love our characters out loud upon our pages." At the very least, the letter writers in this book know that experiencing Salinger's prose is somehow part of a lifelong learning process that may help them overcome false ideas about literature and about themselves.

The literary impact of Salinger's fiction is simply undeniable—his best-selling work has received more critical attention than almost any other post-World War II American writer and it continues to affect generations of readers in profound ways. William Kennedy has clearly tapped Salinger's literary influence and uses a similar family sensibility in his own novels. Kennedy sent us an e-mail explaining Salinger's influence in this way: "I was, like many others, a Salinger fanatic in the 1960s and I reread him frequently, chiefly the Glass family stories, of which I never got enough. The way the family members turned up in the various stories was, like the reappearances of the Compson family members in Faulkner's novels and stories, a strong influence on the structuring of my own work. I keep thinking that one day he will open the vaults and let us have a look at the rest of his work with the Glasses. I hope this is not just my optimism."

The cover blurb on almost any new coming-of-age novel or clever collection of short stories is likely to compare the emerging author with Salinger. Salinger's influence on writing and his appeal for critics continues to grow and find new directions. Poet Molly Peacock uses one sentence from "A Perfect Day for Bananafish" to teach her students the importance and art of syntax. W. P. Kinsella's letter shows what can happen when reading Salinger inspires a reader and writer. In Kinsella's *Shoeless Joe*, not only does Salinger become a main character, but the issue of censoring *The Catcher in the Rye* provides some of Shoeless Joe's best drama. When Kinsella closes his letter by instructing Salinger to "go the distance," readers of *Letters to J. D. Salinger* are able to experience a powerful nexus of fiction and reality—it is as if Kinsella and Salinger can truly understand each other because their fictional emphases have collided with real issues of names and censorship. Jim Harrison feels bolstered by the way Salinger's example showed him that gossip "vaporizes" while good writing remains. And now, in the pages of *Letters to J. D. Salinger* and via the continuing flow of critical books, articles, and Salinger Web pages, we are able to see more clearly that ongoing generations of readers believe that Salinger's work remains important and vital to our literary landscape and to our personal lives.

One of the most frequently asked questions about Salinger is whether he continues to write. Joyce Maynard—the target of Tom Robbins's Zen-like letter—claims to have remembered seeing new manuscripts by Salinger in a "vault sized room." Margaret Salinger reports in her book, *Dream Catcher: A Memoir*, that her father has composed many manuscripts, now color-coded and stored in a cabinet, since his last published story appeared in the June 19, 1965, issue of the *New Yorker*. Salinger himself mentioned "several new Glass stories coming along" on the dust jacket of *Raise High the Roof Beam, Carpenters and Seymour: An Introduction*, although that was in 1963. The issue of Salinger's unpublished writing is quite a mystery—as is the mystery of his present writing habits beyond the known fact that he is a two-fingered typist. Critic Harold Bloom sensed "a curious completeness in his four short books, taken together." Yet there are qualities in Salinger's writing that make readers want to read more or at least reread as much as possible. Only time will tell if there is more Salinger fiction to consider.

Over the years we have learned to content ourselves with Salinger's existing body of work. One of the more interesting ways his fiction continues to thrive is on the Internet. "Bananafish," an e-mail discussion list, began buzzing in 1995 and the number of Salinger pages on the World Wide Web is an astonishing new growth sector of what critic George Steiner has called the "Salinger industry." What does it say about our literary culture when an author's fiction and withdrawal from public life fuels generations of readers into an industry of criticism, a vibrant discussion list (visit Bananafish at http://www.roughdraft.org), a matrix of critical and personal Salinger Web pages, and now a book of unanswered letters? What critical strategies connect this emerging and electronic criticism to the traditional critical response generated from Salinger's fiction?

Whether we experience literature on a printed page or a computer screen our information, ideas, feelings, and the wealth of our living culture still exists in symbolic worlds. But the ways many people experience that literature has changed rapidly as we move into the twenty-first century. Readers are finding more democratic and insightful ways to connect with literature and each other. "Hypertext" is a key word, here and on the Internet, because multilinear links are connecting readers to new texts in powerful and immediate ways. Innovative influences and modes of expression excite new ideas and accelerate some of the traditional ways we respond to words because new configurations of ideas are easily and sometimes instantly available. Looking at the nexus of traditional and hypertext criticism, we can glean valuable insights from the ways criticism, theory, and literature are merging into a more democratic twenty-first century literary experience.

Jay David Bolter's *Writing Space* analyzes the multilinearity of hypertext and writing on the Internet in terms of network dynamics. According to Bolter, traditional connections, links, bridges, meanings, and so forth still exist, but they happen in a free and yet often connected way. According to Bolter, "Each element in this network may be a word, a sentence, a paragraph, and it may be related to as many other elements as the author or the reader (who is also an author) cares to define." In the not too distant future, the multiplicity of ways in which readers may experience Salinger texts will be analyzed in the context of how this criticism has or has not emerged from the printed criticism generated from Salinger's fiction.

Electronic criticism increasingly enables textual transactions. Many of the letters in this book were sent via e-mail and posted to the Letters to

Salinger Web site. Readers and writers using the Internet have tools at their disposal that allow them to find a number of alternate paths through their literary experiences, including conversations with scholars, critics, teachers, students, and friends. Camille Scaysbrook, an Australian writer who submitted her letter via the Letters to Salinger Web site, explains Salinger's relationship with his audience as well as any published critic has when she writes "you make us realize that ultimately the illusion of voice is really the echo of our words, even words that we haven't said yet." And Sanford Pinsker, one of Salinger's most published critics, posted a letter to the Web site that offers humble thanks while also offering the point that he's learned to let Salinger's characters "continue to speak for themselves." Hypertext, as illustrated by a reader and critic showing up on the same Salinger Web page, begins to explain how literature is changing. Carol Osborne and Mike Stracco clearly illustrate in their letter how teaching acumen and e-mail create new possibilities in classrooms. How screens appear and in what order produces multilinearity that is not experienced by turning paper pages or by seeking critical synthesis from articles and books. Hypertextually, the Internet clearly adds new dimensions to litera-ture's critical transactions. The fact that there are many more collaborative paths in and out of texts is one of the most explosive changes in the critical response to Salinger and his fiction. Holden Caulfield may have felt he was outside of his culture and community, but now there is an interna-tional online community of Holden Caulfields!

The Internet has enabled a more democratic mix of ongoing, literary structures. The Bananafish discussion list's Frequently Asked Questions page addresses many of the same critical problems usually clustered in anthologies of Salinger criticism. The Bananafish discussion engages inter-national participants—from academic scholars to adolescents who are reading *The Catcher in the Rye* for the first time. Bananafish participants may read Salinger texts on their own and participate in immediate critical interaction that now seems almost routine to our modern sensibilities. But the traditional world of literary criticism is only beginning to catch up with the speed in which the Internet is changing the reading lives of those outside the academy. The immediacy and ease of critical discussion on Bananafish is not something many of the earlier Salinger critics and readers found typical. Traditional literary thinkers experienced multilinear paths of ideas through letters, in classes, and with papers discussed at occasional scholarly meetings. But the Internet and projects like *Letters to J. D. Salinger* increase the amount, depth, and availability of those paths and create new opportunities for readers and writers to encounter themselves and each other.

Those who have contributed the letters archived at <www.jdsalinger.com> prove overwhelmingly that Salinger's fiction has reached readers around the world in ways that most writers aspire to yet few achieve. It could be that Salinger's vision of love, life, and holiness itself fosters more humane kinds of criticism as well, and there are now better ways for us to understand the meaning of his fiction and the impact of his spirit. Salinger did dedicate his last book to "amateur readers" after all, and he made it clear that he thinks formal critical response to his work is distracting. The author has famously avoided most opportunities to comment on the criticism of his work beyond asking readers to know his ideas and feelings directly from his pages.

There will always be emerging and evolving literary theories, but *Letters to J. D. Salinger* has come along at a time when literature must change profoundly and quickly to ensure that we stay human and connected to the words we love most. As Salinger himself might ask, when critics, writers, readers, teachers and students swim in the same school, is it really a perfect day for bananafish?